HAMILTON

A NEW CITY FOR A NEW MILLENNIUM

By Marvin Ross
Featuring the photography of Mike Grandmaison

Produced in cooperation with the
Hamilton and District Chamber of Commerce

Since 1845

HAMILTON *and District*
Chamber of Commerce
Creating Business Opportunities

HAMILTON

A NEW CITY FOR A NEW MILLENNIUM

■ ■ ■ ■ ■ ■ ■

By Marvin Ross
Featuring the photography of Mike Grandmaison

The Hamilton and District Chamber of Commerce and Community Communications, Inc.

would like to express our gratitude to these companies for their leadership in the development of this book.

NEW CITY OF HAMILTON

Our product is steel. Our strength is people.

 Hamilton Utilities Corporation

Over 100 Years of Love
and Care for Seniors

PHOTO BY MIKE GRANDMAISON.

HAMILTON
A NEW CITY FOR A NEW MILLENNIUM

By Marvin Ross
Featuring the photography of Mike Grandmaison

Community Communications, Inc.
Publisher: Ronald P. Beers

Produced in cooperation with the
Hamilton and District Chamber of Commerce

Staff for *Hamilton: A New City for a New Millennium*

Acquisitions: Henry Beers
Publisher's Sales Associate: Brian Rhodes
Editor in Chief: Wendi L. Lewis
Managing Editor: Kurt R. Niland
Profile Editor: Amanda J. Burbank
Editorial Assistants: Heather Edwards, Rebekah Monson
Design Director: Scott Phillips
Designer: Matt Johnson
Photo Editors: Kurt R. Niland and Matt Johnson
Contract Manager: Christi Stevens
Proofreader: Heather Edwards
Production Manager: Jarrod Stiff
Pre-Press and Separations: Artcraft Graphic Productions
National Sales Manager: Ronald P. Beers
Sales Assistant: Sandra Akers
Acquisitions Coordinator: Angela P. White
Accounting Services: Stephanie Perez

Community Communications, Inc.
Montgomery, Alabama

David M. Williamson, *Chief Executive Officer*
Ronald P. Beers, *President and Publisher*
W. David Brown, *Chief Operating Officer*

© 2000 Community Communications
All Rights Reserved
Published 2000
Printed in Canada
First Edition
Library of Congress Catalog Number: 00-010355
ISBN: 1-58192-025-3

TABLE OF CONTENTS

FOREWORD

Midnight, January 1, 2000, the world welcomed the new millennium.

Midnight, January 1, 2001, it welcomed a brand new city.

Previously known as the Regional Municipality of Hamilton-Wentworth, this family of communities came together to form a "New City of Hamilton," and a powerful new economic unit at the western end of Lake Ontario in Ontario, Canada.

The communities included the towns of Ancaster, Dundas, Flamborough, Glanbrook, the former City of Hamilton and the City of Stoney Creek.

The Hamilton and District Chamber of Commerce has therefore published this book not only to mark the new millennium but also to celebrate the birth of the new city and its promising, prosperous future.

We are grateful to the many organizations and corporations you will find profiled as you turn its pages. Without their support and participation the book would not have been possible.

Known by many as the home of Canada's two largest steel producers, the new city can also boast of numerous corporations who lead the world in technology development, health research, education and environmental advancement.

But there's more. Much more.

A visit to the world-famous Royal Botanical Gardens is a must for every visitor, as is the African Lion Safari, Dundurn Castle, the Canadian Football Hall of Fame, Mountain Brow Lookouts, Confederation Park and our numerous conservation areas.

If you are into arts and culture, then the "New Hamilton" certainly won't disappoint. Hamilton Place, the community's centre for the performing arts, hosts numerous world-famous performers and productions on an annual basis, including our own Opera Hamilton and Philharmonic Orchestra.

Copps Coliseum, our 16,000-seat arena, is the home of the Bulldogs hockey team and stages many other exciting athletic events, musical performances and trade shows.

Those who attend at the DuMaurier Centre for the Performing Arts, home of Theatre Aquarius, the community's professional theatre group, regularly enjoy the works of many of the world's greatest musical composers and playwrights.

The New City is also home to McMaster University, a leading centre of learning in Canada. Mohawk College is recognized throughout the province of Ontario for its excellence in applied arts and technology programs. The New Redeemer University College. The nationally recognized Hillfield-Strathallen private college. Quality public and separate school systems. All of them graduate outstanding scholars on an annual basis.

And our Hamilton Tiger-Cat football team has won the Grey Cup, symbolic of professional football supremacy in Canada, on many occasions.

All of these lifestyle-enhancing assets make the New City of Hamilton one of the most liveable in the world.

A great place in which to live, work, play, invest and visit.

The Hamilton and District Chamber of Commerce

PHOTO BY MIKE GRANDMAISON.

PREFACE

Hamilton was incorporated as a city back in 1846, but in this book we are referring to it as a "new city." We are doing so because on January 1, 2001, it became newly constituted when it amalgamated with its neighbours and all six municipalities go forth as one entity.

Since the creation of the Regional Municipality of Hamilton Wentworth in 1974, Ancaster, Dundas, Flamborough, Glanbrook, Hamilton and Stoney Creek centralized some services, while others remained under the jurisdiction of the local town. With the new millennium, all services come under the new city of close to half a million people, while that sense of community that exists in the various towns still remains. The flag days, heritage days, peach festivals and cactus celebrations, to name a few of the special events, will not disappear.

This new city of Hamilton will draw upon the strengths, expertise and assets of all its parts for a more united effort. Given the wealth of talent and resources that exist, the future should know no bounds for the new Hamilton in this new millennium.

Marvin Ross

Part One

CHAPTER 1

PHYSICAL SETTING

Known throughout the country as an
industrial city of steel mills, blast furnaces
and heavy industry, Hamilton has still
managed to retain and preserve the
beauty of the unique geographical area
in which it is situated.

HAMILTON, A CITY WITH A STEEL REPUTATION FOR MANUFACTURING AND HEAVY
INDUSTRY, IS SITUATED NEAR THE NIAGARA ESCARPMENT, WHICH HAS BEEN
NAMED AS A UNESCO WORLD BIOSPHERE RESERVE ALONG WITH THE
EVERGLADES, THE SERENGETI AND THE GALAPAGOS ISLANDS. TEWS FALLS,
PICTURED HERE, IS JUST ONE FEATURE OF THE ESCARPMENT.
PHOTO BY MIKE GRANDMAISON.

Motorists entering Hamilton from the west or just driving by the city along highway 403 are greeted with a spectacular scene. On one side of the road, they get a panoramic view of Cootes Paradise, the Arboretum at the Royal Botanical Gardens and Princess Point. On the other side is Hamilton Bay with its many sailboats. If they exit the highway and enter the city along Plains Road, they pass over the McQueston Bridge that was originally intended as the main entry gate into the city. Motorists then drive past Dundurn Castle and the Military Museum on their way into the city core.

Motorists coming into the city from the east or just driving by on the QEW over the Burlington Skyway on their way from Toronto to Niagara and the U.S. border have a different view. The skyline they see is that of Stelco, Dofasco and the industrialized north end of the city. Although these mammoth factories are part of the city scape and the environment, they are only a small but important part of Hamilton.

Hamilton has, in fact, earned a reputation for being a "green" area. It is situated in a geographical area known as the Niagara Escarpment. The escarpment, in Hamilton, is called "the mountain." The original city stretches south from the lake to the base of the mountain while the newer part of the city is on the top. This geographical feature stretches for 700 km from Niagara Falls to Tobermory at the tip of the Bruce Peninsula in the North. The Bruce Trail, a series of hiking trails that enable the adventuresome to walk from one end of the escarpment to the other, crosses through the region.

HAMILTON HAS EARNED A REPUTATION FOR BEING A "GREEN" AREA, WITH NATURE AND INDUSTRY COEXISTING THROUGH THE PLACEMENT OF BEAUTIFULLY MAINTAINED PARKS LIKE LAWRENCE PARK THROUGHOUT THE CITY. PHOTO BY MIKE GRANDMAISON.

MOTORISTS ENTERING HAMILTON FROM THE WEST ARE GREETED WITH A SPECTACULAR SCENE FEATURING HAMILTON HARBOUR AND THE ROYAL BOTANICAL GARDENS. PHOTOS BY MIKE GRANDMAISON.

In 1990, the United Nations proclaimed the escarpment a UNESCO World Biosphere Reserve along with the Everglades, the Serengeti and the Galapagos Islands. The lands around Hamilton are nesting sites or staging points for about 225 different species of birds.

It is this unique geographical resource that contributes so much to the beauty of the Hamilton area. The Arboretum that is passed on the way into the city lies near the northern limits of the Carolinian Life Zone. Hickory, sassafras and walnut trees grow and give the area a southern U.S. flavour. In addition, there are the typical beech, maple and hemlock trees that are characteristic of the Great Lakes Region. The hiking trails contain 70 different varieties of trees. In addition, the Arboretum is home to a spectacular lilac festival every spring and numerous other displays of flowers during the appropriate seasons.

Beside the Arboretum and also visible from the highway as you approach the city is Cootes Paradise. This wetland covers 2,000 acres and is surrounded by 21 km of trails. It is named after Captain Thomas Cootes, a British officer stationed at Fort Niagara in the 1780s. He used the area for duck hunting. Archaeological evidence shows that the area was used for hunting and fishing by Natives going as far back as 1500 BC.

Cootes Paradise is designated as a Class I wetland and a provincial area of natural and scientific interest by the Ontario Government, and as an environmentally sensitive area by the city. One of the most unique qualities of this area is its proximity. Many of its trails begin in residential neighborhoods and near public transportation. It is possible to access the trails surrounding the waters from the campus of McMaster University and from the four-lane divided highway known as Cootes Drive Within minutes of the city, hikers can be in dense woods watching deer, geese and other wildlife.

Thanks to the escarpment and the valleys in the area, the Gardens and Cootes Paradise are only two of many scenic and unique locations administered by the conservation authority. Its jurisdiction includes close to 5,000 hectares of land. The Devil's Punch Bowl is the site of a dramatic waterfall that is estimated to have begun to develop 450 million years ago. The Bowl is known to geologists all over the world for its exposed rock strata and is an ideal spot to look out over the city and Hamilton Harbour.

An abandoned rail line has even been converted into the "rail trail" that stretches for 32 km from west Hamilton to the City of Brantford. After leaving the built-up area of Hamilton, the trail winds its way through the Dundas Valley which is home to unique wildlife and vegetation rarely found in Canada. This trail is suitable for walkers, bicyclists, people in wheelchairs and baby strollers.

The other geographical feature of Hamilton is Lake Ontario—one of the six Great Lakes. Fifty Point is a 76-hectare park on the water with a marina, camping and fine dining. Visitors can fish for salmon in the lake or for trout in the stocked ponds in the park. A clean beach and picnic and camping areas are also available for visitors. Farther east along the lake is the boardwalk and the Wild Water Works playground at Van Wagner's Beach and Confederation Park. ■

Motorists coming into the city from the east or diving by on the QEW over the Burlington Skyway have a view of Hamilton's industrial face, featuring Stelco, Dofasco and the industrialized north end of the city. Top photo by Mike Grandmaison. Bottom photo by Sandy Bell.

BAYFRONT PARK PROVIDES AN IDEAL SETTING FOR A RELAXING STROLL TO UNWIND FROM A DAY'S
STRESSES, OR A HEARTY WALK OR JOG FOR BETTER HEALTH. PHOTOS BY MIKE GRANDMAISON.

HAMILTON IS CENTRALLY LOCATED TO MAJOR MARKETS IN EASTERN CANADA, NEW YORK, MICHIGAN, PENNSYLVANIA AND OHIO, AND IS AN IDEAL SPOT TO OBTAIN RAW MATERIALS AND TO SHIP GOODS TO MARKET. PHOTO BY MIKE GRANDMAISON.

AMCAN CASTINGS LIMITED

AMCAN Castings, established in Hamilton in 1936, offers ample proof of the benefits that can be derived for both the company and its employees from using the new technology and robotics. The company, which designs and manufactures high-pressure aluminum die cast parts for the automotive industry, has increased its sales from $20 million per year in 1992 to a projected $240 million in 2000. This increase in productivity through automation was completed with no reduction in its workforce, with the help of its workers and with no labour disputes. Along the way, it won community awards for its business excellence and its contributions to the community. ∎

HAMILTON'S NEIGHBOURHOODS REPRESENT A RANGE OF STYLES AND TASTES. SUBURBAN, DOWNTOWN OR RURAL LIVING, NEW HOMES OR OLD, THERE ARE COMMUNITIES WHERE ANYONE CAN FEEL AT HOME. PHOTOS BY MIKE GRANDMAISON.

HAMILTON HEALTH SCIENCES CORPORATION

The Hamilton Health Sciences Corporation provides comprehensive services to all age groups and for all medical conditions. It is the only hospital in Ontario that provides services to its patients from preconception in its Invitro Fertilization Clinic through to chronic and palliative care. HHSC also has the distinction as being one of the largest academic health service facilities in Canada through its affiliation with the Faculty of Health Sciences at McMaster University. Because of this affiliation, HHSC also has a strong focus on teaching and research. This partnership with the medical school has enabled HHSC to attract some of the best and most innovative health-care professionals in the world. ∎

HAMILTON UTILITIES CORPORATION

Hamilton Hydro customers have always benefited from one of the most efficient hydro systems in the province while being provided a safe, reliable and cost-effective service. Today, entering into a deregulated environment, the multi-utility company is a vibrant example of successfully balancing public interest with that of a commercial corporation. Providing state-of-the-art fibre-optic communication links, demonstrated outsourcing skills as well as maintaining a strong core distribution company will allow Hamilton Utilities Corporation and its subsidiary companies to continue growing within and outside the city's boundaries. Their goal is to be recognized as the leader in the delivery of municipal utility services with their customers saying they are receiving best value. ■

CONFEDERATION PARK IS LOCATED ALONG LAKE ONTARIO, ONE OF THE SIX GREAT LAKES.
VISITORS CAN TREK ALONG THE BOARDWALK OR BEACHFRONT, AND ENJOY THE WILD WATER WORKS
PLAYGROUND AT VAN WAGNER'S BEACH. PHOTO BY MIKE GRANDMAISON.

NEW CITY OF HAMILTON

Judged to be one of the best places in Ontario to live, Hamilton and its surrounding municipalities are well positioned to be successful. The newly amalgamated municipality with over 500,000 people, has many strong assets including: an excellent location, available and reasonably priced industrial land, a highly skilled workforce and a quality of life that is second to none. In addition to a strong and vibrant steel industry, the city is home to numerous other manufacturing industries, first-rate hospitals, educational and research facilities and a geography that provides the beauty of the countryside within easy access. ∎

DOFASCO

Dofasco is entering the new millennium with a great deal of optimism and a greater competitive strength than at any time in its history thanks to its innovative approach of producing value-added steel products designed to solve the needs of its customers. In the past decade, over $2 billion has been invested in new technology and facilities in Hamilton, and productivity has increased over 50 per cent. Fifty per cent of its current products were not even available 10 years ago. Today, as has been the case since 1912, Dofasco's product is steel, its strength is people and its home is Hamilton. ■

THE NIAGARA ESCARPMENT STRETCHES FOR 700 KILOMETRES FROM NIAGARA FALLS TO TOBERMORY AT THE TIP OF THE BRUCE PENINSULA IN THE NORTH. A NUMBER OF SMALLER FALLS ARE SCATTERED ALONG THE ESCARPMENT. PHOTO BY MIKE GRANDMAISON.

MOHAWK COLLEGE

Mohawk College is proud of the accomplishments and innovations that have been achieved since its inception in 1967. Among the first group of colleges created by the Ontario government to provide a new level of post-secondary education for students, Mohawk was the first school to provide cooperative education programs. It now has the largest apprenticeship program in the Province. Mohawk was also one of the first colleges to implement a regular program review. Over 1,000 people from various businesses and industries act as advisors for programs. This helps to ensure that student skills respond to the needs of industry. ■

HAMILTON HARBOUR ON HAMILTON BAY IS THE MOORING SITE FOR A NUMBER OF SAILBOATS AND OTHER PLEASURE CRAFT. PHOTO BY MIKE GRANDMAISON.

TUBE-MAC® INDUSTRIES

Operating on quality assurances designed to meet ISO 9001, Tube-Mac® designs, manufactures and supplies non-welded piping systems for hydraulic lines, lubrication and grease lines, paint and ink lines. Tube-Mac® Industries (TMI®) supplies complete piping packages including pipes, hoses, clamps, ball valves and custom manifold blocks. Tube-Mac® offers AutoCad layout drawings, field supervision, special installation equipment, oil flushing and oil analysis of TMI® piping systems. TMI® piping systems require no welding, so there is no need for acid pickling, flushing and the disposal of waste fluids that are hazardous to the environment. ■

THE DAYS AT BAYFRONT PARK ARE FILLED WITH SUNSHINE AND ACTIVITY BEFORE THE EVENING BRINGS ITS PEACEFUL BEAUTY TO THE LANDSCAPE. PHOTOS BY MIKE GRANDMAISON.

THE ESCARPMENT, IN HAMILTON, IS CALLED "THE MOUNTAIN." THE ORIGINAL CITY STRETCHES SOUTH FROM THE LAKE TO THE BASE OF THE MOUNTAIN, WHILE THE NEWER PART OF THE CITY IS ON THE TOP. PHOTO BY MIKE GRANDMAISON.

St. Peter's Health System

St. Peter's Health System is committed to providing a continuum of service for seniors and care for the chronically ill. This integrated system of care for the elderly and chronically ill is the first of its kind in the province. St. Peter's will ensure that they continue to receive the best possible care and that St. Peter's 110 years of expertise continues to improve their quality of life. ■

PRICEWATERHOUSECOOPERS LLP

PricewaterhouseCoopers' vision is to be the best professional services firm in the world, as measured by the markets and clients it serves and by its people. As the result of internal growth and a series of mergers, the most recent between PriceWaterhouse and Coopers & Lybrand in 1998, the Hamilton office has grown to seven partners and a staff of 100. The firm continues to enjoy a well-earned reputation for excellence, innovative client services and professional leadership. Thanks to its international presence, the company is able to provide its local clients with appropriate expertise and experience, as required, of any one of its 150,000 professionals in its offices located in 150 countries around the world. ■

PHOTOS BY MIKE GRANDMAISON.

ENTERING THE CITY ALONG PLAINS ROAD, VISITORS PASS OVER THE McQUESTON BRIDGE THAT WAS ORIGINALLY INTENDED AS THE MAIN ENTRY GATE INTO THE CITY. PHOTOS BY MIKE GRANDMAISON.

St. Joseph's Hospital and St. Joseph's Villa

St. Joseph's Hospital is a 400-plus (soon to grow to more than 700) bed teaching hospital affiliated with the Faculty of Health Sciences at McMaster University and Mohawk College.

It is dedicated to providing compassionate, sensitive care to its patients and their families and to achieving excellence in health care through an on-going commitment to education and research.

St. Joseph's Villa and Estates, Dundas, is home to 564 seniors. Additionally the Villa's continuum of care model serves 340 seniors. Built on the 120-year history of the Sisters of St. Joseph, the Villa has been recognized locally, nationally and internationally with quality awards. These awards were presented from *Hamilton Spectator*, the Fraser Institute/Donner Foundation and ISO 9002. ∎

McMaster University

McMaster University offers 141 undergraduate degrees in six faculties—humanities, business, engineering, science, social sciences and health sciences. The graduate school supports 38 masters and 28 doctoral programs and an MD degree. Graduates excel in all fields and count among their better-known alumni: Roberta Bondar, the Canadian astronaut; The Honourable Lincoln Alexander, a former federal cabinet minister and lieutenant governor of Ontario; Ivan Reitman, the film director; and Martin Short, actor and comedian. Among McMaster's illustrious faculty of over 1,100 is a co-winner of the 1994 Nobel Prize for Physics—Dr. Bertram Brockhouse. The world-renowned Faculty of Health Sciences pioneered problem-based learning for its medical students since adopted by Harvard. ∎

ALTHOUGH HAMILTON'S MOST VISIBLE INDUSTRY CAN BE SEEN IN THE MAMMOTH FACTORIES THAT MAKE UP THE CITYSCAPE, AGRICULTURAL ENDEAVORS BY MENNONITE FARMERS, LOCAL WINERIES, AND OTHERS ARE AN IMPORTANT PART OF THE CITY'S DIVERSE ECONOMIC PICTURE. PHOTOS BY MIKE GRANDMAISON.

CHAPTER 2

THE ECONOMY

When the early pioneers first set down roots

at the extreme western end of Lake Ontario

and founded the settlement of Hamilton,

they probably did not realize that

they had chosen a spot with ideal

conditions for long-term growth—

Location, Location, Location.

■ ■ ■ ■ ■ ■ ■

THERE ARE AN ESTIMATED 20 MILLION CUSTOMERS WITHIN A ONE-DAY DRIVE OF
HAMILTON. PHOTO BY MIKE GRANDMAISON.

It wasn't until 1813 that the settlement even became large enough to be incorporated as a village. However, with the completion of the Burlington Canal in 1832 and the arrival of lake ships, the community began to grow so that by 1833 it became a town. Growth continued and Hamilton, named after local farmer George Hamilton, graduated to city status in 1846—a year after the merchants had set up the local Board of Trade which was to eventually become the Chamber of Commerce. Thanks to the coming of the Great Western Railway in the 1850s, Hamilton expanded even more.

With its access to shipping on the Great Lakes and its rail connections, the city possessed the key ingredients for industrial growth. Although today Hamilton is known throughout Canada as the Steel City, the steel industry is just one of many in a highly diversified economy that keeps pace with technological advances. During the 1880s and prior to the coming of steel, Hamilton was known as the "electric city." Hamilton was quick to embrace the use of this new energy source which was becoming increasingly more available thanks to the newly developing hydroelectric generators nearby. Westinghouse opened a plant in Hamilton because of the city's use of electric power.

Early use of electricity, though, was just one of many new developments that the city embraced and that helped attract other industry to the area. The first telephone exchange in the entire British Empire was set up in Hamilton. In 1881, Canada's first public telephone was established in the city while the first long-distance call made in Canada was from Hamilton to nearby Dundas.

A few decades earlier in 1860, the Prince of Wales, who later became Edward VII, officially opened the city's new waterworks system that was recognized as the country's best. Water was pumped from Lake Ontario and the city set up a Board of Water Commissioners in 1861 to manage the new convenience. Thanks to all of these developments, more and more industries began to settle in the area. Then, in 1912, because of the easy access to a good supply of raw materials through the harbour, Clifton Sherman arrived from the U.S. to establish Dominion Steel Casting Ltd.—a forerunner of Dofasco and today one of the most profitable steel companies in North America. With the coming of the automobile and the development of highways, Hamilton's strategic location improved even more. The city is centrally located to major markets in Eastern Canada, New York, Michigan, Pennsylvania and Ohio and in an ideal spot to obtain raw materials and to ship goods to market. There are an estimated 20 million customers within a one-day drive of the city.

The John C. Munro International Airport is another positive for business in the area. The airport is home to sorting facilities for UPS and Purolator, and there are plans for the establishment of a sorting centre for Federal Express as well. As a result, the airport is the major cargo handling resource for Eastern Canada. This has resulted in a substantial increase in industrial development in the lands adjacent to the airport.

Passenger travel is also expanding as airlines are now starting to use Hamilton as an alternative to the busy Lester B. Pearson International Airport that serves Toronto. U.S. Air Express operates regular flights out of Hamilton to its hubs in Pittsburgh. There, passengers can connect to

HAMILTON IS KNOWN THROUGHOUT CANADA AS THE STEEL CITY, ALTHOUGH TODAY THE STEEL INDUSTRY IS JUST ONE OF MANY IN A HIGHLY DIVERSIFIED ECONOMY THAT KEEPS PACE WITH TECHNOLOGICAL ADVANCES. PHOTO BY MIKE GRANDMAISON.

HAMILTON, NAMED AFTER FARMER GEORGE HAMILTON, GRADUATED TO CITY STATUS IN 1846—
A YEAR AFTER THE MERCHANTS HAD SET UP THE LOCAL BOARD OF TRADE WHICH WAS TO EVENTUALLY
BECOME THE CHAMBER OF COMMERCE. PHOTO BY MIKE GRANDMAISON.

WITH AN ABUNDANCE OF NATURALLY RUNNING AND FALLING WATER, HYDROELECTRIC GENERATORS WERE CONSTRUCTED NEARBY. THE POWER THEY GENERATED MADE HAMILTON THE "ELECTRIC CITY" IN THE EARLY 1800S. PHOTO BY MIKE GRANDMAISON.

HAMILTON IS A CITY OF FIRSTS - THE FIRST TELEPHONE EXCHANGE IN THE ENTIRE BRITISH EMPIRE WAS SET UP IN HAMILTON, AND IN 1881 CANADA'S FIRST PUBLIC TELEPHONE WAS ESTABLISHED IN THE CITY. A FEW DECADES EARLIER, IN 1860, THE PRINCE OF WALES OFFICIALLY OPENED THE CITY'S NEW WATERWORKS SYSTEM THAT WAS RECOGNIZED AS THE COUNTRY'S BEST, AND THE CITY SET UP A BOARD OF WATER COMMISSIONERS IN 1861 TO MANAGE THE NEW CONVENIENCE. PHOTO BY MIKE GRANDMAISON.

numerous other destinations. The Canadian carrier, WestJet Air, also provides regular flights to its destinations across Canada. Hamilton is now the new Eastern hub for Westjet, which handles about 250,000 passengers a year out of John C. Munro.

As we start out in the new millennium, a new form of transportation or communication is evolving and that is high speed fibre optic cabling and the internet. In keeping with its history of embracing new technologies to encourage growth and prosperity for its citizens, Hamilton is leading the way in this area as well.

Hamilton is now a "wired city," thanks to the efforts of the Hydro Commission. The system that Hydro installed for its own internal data communications use has sufficient capacity to enable local businesses to communicate with each other and with partners around the world. The newly established Centre for Minimal Access Surgery at St. Joseph's Hospital (the first of its kind in Canada), uses this system to video conference with surgical centres across Canada and all around the world.

Hamilton surgical students are able to watch, learn and communicate with surgical experts as they operate while Hamilton surgeons can use the facilities to train surgical students in other places.

Meanwhile, Dofasco is now using the Internet to conduct its steel business and McMaster has established an MBA program to train people in the rapidly expanding business of e-commerce. The Faculty of Health Sciences has become a world leader in the use of the Internet for medicine and health care through its Health Information and Research Unit. One of its stated goals is to ensure that the doctor-patient relationship is strengthened rather than weakened with the easy availability of more patient information. The Greater Hamilton Technology Enterprise Centre was established by the city to help foster the growth of these new high-tech or knowledgebased businesses as they are sometimes called.

Tourism is another high growth area for the Hamilton economy thanks again to its geographical position. Aside from the natural beauty of the area, Hamilton has been described as the hub of a wheel because of its location. Tourists and tour groups can make Hamilton their home base. They can take in the local sites, benefit from hotels that are more reasonably priced than those in Toronto or Niagara and take day trips to Toronto, Niagara, the Shaw Festival, Stratford and the Shakespearean Festival, the Mennonite farmers market in St. Jacobs and explore local wineries. The western end of the Ontario wine district begins just east of Hamilton.

In addition to all of these features, Hamilton still has a substantial amount of serviced land that is ready to be developed and at prices that are quite competitive. Added to all of this is a highly trained and co-operative workforce with one of the lowest unemployment rates in the country. These factors all translate into the potential for considerable growth and opportunity in the years to come. ■

HAMILTON HAS A SUBSTANTIAL AMOUNT OF SERVICED LAND THAT IS READY TO BE DEVELOPED, AT PRICES THAT ARE QUITE COMPETITIVE, AS WELL AS A HIGHLY TRAINED AND CO-OPERATIVE WORKFORCE, AND ONE OF THE LOWEST UNEMPLOYMENT RATES IN THE COUNTRY. PHOTO BY MIKE GRANDMAISON.

ABOVE: THE JOHN C. MUNRO INTERNATIONAL AIRPORT IS A POSITIVE FOR BUSINESS IN THE AREA, AS THE HOME TO SORTING FACILITIES FOR UPS AND PUROLATOR, WITH PLANS ON THE HORIZON FOR THE ESTABLISHMENT OF A SORTING CENTRE FOR FEDERAL EXPRESS. THE AIRPORT IS THE MAJOR CARGO HANDLING RESOURCE FOR EASTERN CANADA. PHOTO BY MIKE GRANDMAISON.

BELOW: HAMILTON'S VARIED TRANSPORTATION OPTIONS - INCLUDING ROADS, RAIL, AIR, AND WATER - MAKE IT THE IDEAL LOCATION FOR SHIPPING GOODS TO MARKET THROUGHOUT EASTERN CANADA AND THE UNITED STATES. PHOTO BY MIKE GRANDMAISON.

THE HAMILTON HARBOUR IS THE FOUNDATION OF THE CITY'S BUSINESS ECONOMY. IN 1912, RECOGNIZING THE HARBOUR AS THE SOURCE FOR EASY ACCESS TO A GOOD SUPPLY OF RAW MATERIALS, CLIFTON SHERMAN ARRIVED FROM THE U.S. TO ESTABLISH DOMINION STEEL CASTING LTD. - A FORERUNNER OF DOFASCO AND TODAY ONE OF THE MOST PROFITABLE STEEL COMPANIES IN NORTH AMERICA. PHOTO BY MIKE GRANDMAISON.

WITH THE COMING OF THE AUTOMOBILE AND THE DEVELOPMENT OF THE HIGHWAYS, HAMILTON'S STRATEGIC LOCATION IMPROVED EVEN MORE. THE CITY IS CENTRALLY LOCATED TO MAJOR MARKETS IN EASTERN CANADA, NEW YORK, MICHIGAN, PENNSYLVANIA AND OHIO. ADDITIONALLY, WITHIN THE CITY, A WELL-STRUCTURED AND ACCESSIBLE MASS TRANSIT SYSTEM GETS RESIDENTS WHERE THEY NEED TO GO. PHOTO BY MIKE GRANDMAISON.

TOURISM IS A HIGH-GROWTH AREA FOR THE HAMILTON ECONOMY THANKS TO ITS GEOGRAPHICAL
POSITION. PHOTO BY MIKE GRANDMAISON.

ASIDE FROM THE NATURAL BEAUTY OF THE AREA, HAMILTON HAS BEEN DESCRIBED AS THE HUB OF A WHEEL BECAUSE OF ITS LOCATION. TOURISTS AND TOUR GROUPS CAN MAKE HAMILTON THEIR HOME BASE, EXPLORING THE LOCAL SITES, BENEFITING FROM HOTEL RATES THAT ARE OFTEN MORE REASONABLY PRICED THAN THOSE IN TORONTO OR NIAGARA, AND TAKING DAY TRIPS TO THOSE TWO CITIES AS WELL AS THE SHAW FESTIVAL, STRATFORD AND THE SHAKESPEAREAN FESTIVAL, THE MENNONITE FARMERS MARKET IN ST. JACOBS, AND LOCAL WINERIES. PHOTOS BY MIKE GRANDMAISON.

CHAPTER 3

HEALTH CARE & EDUCATION

It seems somewhat fitting that the area in which Sir William Osler grew up should have such advanced health care and resources. Osler was one of Canada's and the United States' most famous physicians. Originally a professor of medicine at McGill University in Montreal, he went on to become one of the founders of Baltimore's highly acclaimed Johns Hopkins University Medical School.

THE CITY'S CULTURE AND RECREATION DEPARTMENT PROVIDES EXTENSIVE ACTIVITIES FOR CHILDREN OF ALL AGES, SUCH AS SWIMMING, DANCING, ARTS AND CRAFTS. PHOTO BY MIKE GRANDMAISON.

A STONE MONUMENT HONOURS THE ACHIEVEMENTS OF MEDICAL PIONEER AND ONE-TIME LOCAL
RESIDENT SIR WILLIAM OSLER. PHOTO BY MIKE GRANDMAISON.

His textbook—*The Principles and Practices of Medicine* published in 1892—was considered to be the first great textbook of modern medicine. Osler ended his career as Regius Professorship of Medicine at Oxford University, but was raised in Dundas where he attended Central Public School. That elementary school is still instructing students today and is not far from the monument built in the town in his honour.

Today, Hamilton is the centre of the Ontario Ministry of Health's Central West Area. Its hospitals provide specialized care not only for the city but for the catchment area stretching from Niagara Falls to north of Guelph and from Oakville through to Brantford and Simcoe. It serves a population of about 2 million people. Hamilton is home to the Hamilton Health Sciences Corporation, St. Joseph's and St. Peter's Hospitals, and the Hamilton Regional Cancer Centre.

The Children's Hospital and its Chedoke Child and Family Program are part of the Health Sciences Corporation. In addition to the normal services provided by a hospital for children, the child and family program is a rather unique feature of the hospital that ensures children receive comprehensive, coordinated services regardless of their needs or the complexity of their problems. It stresses family-centred care in order to deal with both the needs of the child and the family.

HAMILTON IS HOME TO THE HAMILTON HEALTH SCIENCES CORPORATION, ST. JOSEPH'S AND ST.
PETER'S HOSPITALS, AND THE HAMILTON REGIONAL CANCER CENTRE (PICTURED ABOVE). PHOTO BY
MIKE GRANDMAISON.

THE FACULTY OF HEALTH SCIENCES AT MCMASTER UNIVERSITY HAS BECOME A WORLD LEADER IN
THE USE OF THE INTERNET FOR MEDICINE AND HEALTH CARE THROUGH ITS HEALTH INFORMATION AND
RESEARCH UNIT. ONE OF ITS STATED GOALS IS TO ENSURE THAT THE DOCTOR-PATIENT RELATIONSHIP IS
STRENGTHENED RATHER THAN WEAKENED WITH THE EASY AVAILABILITY OF MORE PATIENT INFORMATION.
PHOTO BY MIKE GRANDMAISON.

The program is involved in assessment, diagnosis, treatment, education and research for a wide variety of developmental, physical, communication, behavioural and emotional problems that afflict children and adolescents. The program cares for children with autism, developmental delay, hyperactivity, language and learning disorders, cleft lip and palate, and neuromuscular diseases. When a child with a disability is ready to enter the regular school system, staff in the program work with the teachers and the neighbourhood school to develop learning plans appropriate to that child's needs and abilities.

Nineteen separate health care disciplines are represented on the staff of the program, all of whom are highly committed to providing the best care possible "in the community where they are most needed and where they can do the most good." Staff are also very involved in research and provide educational opportunities for others. Approximately 300 workshops, courses and lectures are given each year while students in child psychiatry, psychology, social work, pediatrics and other disciplines gain hands-on knowledge from their involvement with the programs.

Thanks to the hospitals, their close affiliation to the medical school at McMaster, and the ability of both to attract world-class medical researchers to Hamilton, residents have an additional benefit from

HAMILTON IS INVOLVED IN THE TESTING OF NEW TREATMENTS FOR OSTEOPOROSIS, ALZHEIMER'S DISEASE, HEART PROBLEMS, HIGH BLOOD PRESSURE AND A HOST OF OTHER MEDICAL PROBLEMS. NOT ONLY CAN HAMILTONIANS HELP WITH THE ADVANCEMENT OF MEDICAL TREATMENT, BUT THEY CAN BE AMONG THE FIRST TO BENEFIT FROM THESE NEW DISCOVERIES. PHOTO BY MIKE GRANDMAISON.

health care. Hamilton is becoming a global centre for the clinical evaluation of new drugs and treatments for a wide range of medical problems. As part of the process to ensure that a new drug is both safe and effective, clinical trials are conducted with thousands of people.

In this kind of research, half the people in a trial get the drug and half get a fake pill or placebo. The outcomes and side effects from the two groups are compared to determine if the new drug works. In order to prevent biases from influencing the findings, no one knows who received the actual drug and who received the placebo. Numerous drug trials are being carried out in Hamilton and the city is now home to the new Clinical Research Institute.

Hamilton is involved in the testing of new treatments for osteoporosis, Alzheimer's Disease, heart problems, high blood pressure and a host of other medical problems. Not only can Hamiltonians help with the advancement of medical treatment, but they can be among the first to benefit from these new discoveries.

THE HAMILTON PUBLIC SCHOOL BOARD HAS 137 SCHOOLS IN THE AREA, OF WHICH NINETEEN ARE AT THE SECONDARY LEVEL. THERE ARE 3,200 TEACHERS FOR 60,000 PUPILS. THE SEPARATE SCHOOL BOARD HAS A TOTAL OF SIXTY SCHOOLS, OF WHICH SIX ARE SECONDARY, AND A TOTAL ENROLLMENT OF 28,000. THERE ARE ABOUT 1,000 TEACHERS IN THIS SYSTEM. PHOTOS BY MIKE GRANDMAISON.

Hamilton families with young children have a wide range of options to acquire the type of education they want their children to have. At the preschool level, there are numerous choices for nursery schools and day care centres ranging from co-operatives to those that utilize specific educational philosophies.

The city Culture and Recreation Department provides extensive activities for children of all ages, such as swimming, dancing, arts and crafts. Many of these programs are designed for children as young as three years old. Special programs are also arranged for Halloween, Christmas and March Break.

The Hamilton public school board has 137 schools in the area, of which 19 are at the secondary level. There are 3,200 teachers for 60,000 pupils. The separate school board has a total of 60 schools, of which six are secondary, and a total enrollment of 28,000. There are about 1,000 teachers in this system. Both boards also provide substantial continuing education courses for adults. In addition to the public and separate school systems, families also have the option of having their children educated in private and/or religious schools. People have no end of choice in Hamilton when it comes to ensuring that their children are educated according to their wishes and principals.

BOTH MCMASTER UNIVERSITY AND MOHAWK COLLEGE HAVE FORGED STRONG TIES WITH LOCAL INDUSTRY. MOHAWK WAS THE FIRST COLLEGE IN ONTARIO TO PROVIDE CO-OP EDUCATION SO THAT ITS STUDENTS COULD LEARN ON THE JOB. PHOTOS BY MIKE GRANDMAISON.

A STRONG, DYNAMIC LEVEL OF POST SECONDARY EDUCATION IS AN IMPORTANT INCENTIVE TO THE ECONOMIC DEVELOPMENT OF THE AREA. PHOTO BY MIKE GRANDMAISON.

Of particular advantage both to families and to businesses in the area is the existence of a large number of specialized trade schools and a first-rate community college and university. Young people in Hamilton do not have to leave in order to acquire the education they want while businesses are assured of a steady flow of highly skilled graduates who can easily step into jobs.

This strong, dynamic level of post-secondary education is an important incentive to the economic development of the area. Both McMaster University and Mohawk College have forged strong ties with local industry. Mohawk was the first college in Ontario to provide co-op education so that its students could actually learn on the job. By maintaining close ties with the major employers and McMaster, the college is able to provide courses that are relevant to both its students and to industry.

McMaster University, meanwhile, is home to the Centre for Manufacturing and the Centre for Steel Research both of which enhance the traditional economic base of the city. It is also forging ahead into new areas with the establishment of an e-commerce MBA program to take advantage of the rapidly developing internet market and has set up a very highly sophisticated mock stock exchange in its business school. ■

CHAPTER 4

ARTS & ATTRACTIONS

Hamilton is more than just a steel town.

It is, according to the Players Guild, "a theatre

town," and has been since at least the 1820s

when plays were performed in a small room

off Lover's Lane. Since those days, Hamilton

has been home to at least one, and usually

more, amateur theatre groups.

■ ■ ■ ■ ■ ■

THE IRVING ZUCKER SCULPTURE COURT AT THE ART GALLERY OF HAMILTON
NOT ONLY COMPLEMENTS THE GALLERY'S SUBSTANTIAL ART COLLECTION, IT ALSO
PROVIDES AN IDEAL SPOT FOR BUSY DOWNTOWN OFFICE WORKERS TO HAVE A
LEISURELY LUNCH ON A SUNNY DAY. PHOTO BY MIKE GRANDMAISON.

In October of 1875, the Garrick Club marked its first amateur production of *David Garrick* and *Raising the Wind*. From 1875 until the advent of World War I, this group put on countless plays and, in the process, raised money for the Girl's Home, the Home of the Friendless, the Police Benefit Fund, the Hamilton Cricket Club and the Victoria Order of Nurses. In 1929, one of its early members resurrected the group as the Players Guild. After putting on performances in various locations throughout the city, they acquired their own building in 1951 and then added a rehearsal hall to it in 1958.

Today they put on performances at the Sir John A. MacDonald Theatre for which they were instrumental in raising money. They also run an active workshop program for people interested in becoming involved in the theatre. Numerous Canadian actors got their first start in the theatre through these workshops.

The Dundas Little Theatre is another of the area's active theatre groups where those who love live performances can either enjoy a show at the company's venue in Dundas or participate by acting or working behind stage. This theatre group has been entertaining people for over 40 years. A newer entrant into amateur theatre is the Great

TOP: THE PEOPLE OF HAMILTON LOVE MUSIC IN ALL OF ITS FORMS, AS TESTIFIED BY THE NUMBER OF THEATRES, CONCERT HALLS, AND MUSICAL GROUPS AND EVENTS PRESENT IN THE CITY. PHOTO BY SANDY BELL.

BOTTOM: WHEN IT COMES TO MUSIC, HAMILTON'S PRIDE IS HAMILTON PLACE, WHICH IS ONE OF NORTH AMERICA'S MOST EXPANSIVE AND ACOUSTICALLY SUPERIOR HALLS. PHOTO MIKE GRANDMAISON.

Big Theatre Company. It is a full-time children's and young people's theatre company and theatre school in the area. Some of the other amateur groups in the city are the Ancaster Community Theatre, the Binbrook Little Theatre, Hamilton Theatre Inc., Waterdown Amateur Theatre and the Stoney Creek Little Theatre.

Of course, Hamilton also has its own professional theatre group in Theatre Aquarius, which offers a variety of different plays and musicals at the newly constructed du Maurier Centre. In addition to plays by top-name authors and the annual family-oriented holiday musical at Christmas, the company has its Stage Write Series. This is a group of plays written by up and coming Canadian authors and performed in the more intimate surroundings of the smaller studio theatre at Hamilton Place.

Recently, an old time vaudeville hall was reopened to provide Hamiltonians with good dinner theatre. The Redmill Theatre at 80 James St. N in the heart of the downtown district was first opened in 1907 as a movie theatre, vaudeville house and penny arcade. Closed since 1978, it is now back and providing dinner, drinks and entertaining shows with the goal to again make it a lively place like it was back in the Roaring Twenties.

When it comes to music, Hamilton's pride is Hamilton Place—one of North America's most expansive and acoustically superior halls. It is specifically designed to provide optimal acoustical results for both the spoken word and musical presentations. The Great Hall's most unique feature is a retracting 6,500 square-foot stage that enables it to provide two stage formats. When it is forward, concerts can be played within the hall itself. When it is back, drama can be performed behind a proscenium.

In addition to visiting performers, Hamilton Place is home to Opera Hamilton, the New Hamilton Orchestra, The Bach-Elgar Choir and the Geritol Follies. The Bach-Elgar Choir has been described as the "definitive choral voice of the city," and its company of 100 voices has been renowned since 1905 performing classics, pop, show tunes and folk. The Geritol Follies is an internationally acclaimed group of seniors who put on variety shows with as much zest and spirit as performers half their age.

THE HAMILTON MUSEUM OF STEAM AND TECHNOLOGY SHOWCASES THE TOOLS, MACHINERY, AND TECHNOLOGY THAT POWERED CANADA'S INDUSTRIAL REVOLUTION. PHOTO BY MIKE GRANDMAISON.

THE CANADIAN WARPLANE HERITAGE MUSEUM, LOCATED IN THE JOHN C. MUNROE INTERNATIONAL AIRPORT, IS CANADA'S FINEST AVIATION MUSEUM. PHOTO BY MIKE GRANDMAISON.

The Boris Brott Summer Music Festival attracts tourists to the city from all over North America. This is one of the city's foremost musical events and includes concerts, lectures, recitals and a host of other activities. The National Academy Orchestra, conducted by Boris Brott, performs classical, chamber, pops, jazz and big band music.

For over 30 years, the Te Deum Orchestra and Singers have been performing baroque music in Hamilton and Toronto. Performances are in both Toronto and Hamilton's Christ Church Cathedrals. In addition, Copps Coliseum is more than just a hockey rink. Headline musical acts from around the world from the Backstreet Boys to rock and roll greats have appeared here and entertained local fans.

The Hamilton Art Gallery, founded in 1914, is the third largest in Ontario with over 8,000 pieces of European, Canadian and American Art. It houses Canada's finest collection of Canadian historical, modernist and contemporary art. It also has a strong European and American collection along with an outdoor sculpture court, which is an ideal spot for busy downtown office workers to have a leisurely lunch on a sunny day.

The gallery puts on numerous shows by current regional and Canadian artists as well as hosting travelling shows of national or international artists. In addition to the exhibits, it also has an active public program. There are specialized programs for families with young children, tours of the gallery collection, special programs for those over 55 and regular classes for people of all ages and with varying interests.

Aside from the numerous private galleries in the area that showcase local talent, there is also the Dundas Valley School of Art. The school was founded over 35 years ago and, in 1970, moved into a heritage building dating from 1860. This old factory originally had been the Canada Screw Works and then an ammunition factory during World War I. Today, it houses 27,000 square feet of studio space and the Dofasco Gallery, which showcases the works of the school's staff, students and local artists.

The school maintains an active part-time program of instruction for about 4,000 students ranging in age from four to seniors. In partnership with McMaster University, it also provides a three-year diploma program for full-time students. The highlight of its program is its annual art sale and auction held every spring.

The Hamilton area is also home to many artisans and craft people. In both the spring and fall, many of them open their studios to visitors and allow people the opportunity to talk with them about art, to see how they produce their craft and, of course, to buy directly from the artist.

One of Hamilton's most recognized landmarks is Dundurn Castle, a national historic site that illustrates the life and times of Sir Allan Napier MacNab who lived from 1798 to 1862. Dundurn is Gaelic for "fort on the water" and the home, which was designed as a Regency-style villa and completed in 1835, sits majestically overlooking Hamilton Bay. It received the nickname of "castle" from the local citizens and, with its gardens, grounds and various outbuildings, was considered one of the finest estates in Ontario.

Today it is restored to the year 1855 and its 40-plus rooms have been furnished to show the contrast in the living conditions between a prominent family and that of their servants. MacNab was a lawyer, landowner, railway magnate and Premier of the United Canadas from 1845 to 1856. MacNab was declared a "boy hero" for his role in the War of 1812 and was knighted by Queen Victoria for his support of the royalist forces in the Rebellion of 1837.

Located on the grounds of Dundurn Park is the Hamilton Military Museum, which displays military history from the War of 1812 to the Second World War. Artifacts from the War of 1812 battleships, *The Hamilton* and *The Scourge*, are on display. The grounds are part of

Burlington Heights—a strategic military post during the War of 1812. It is now another National Historic Site.

Also a National Historic Site is Whitehern in the downtown core behind City Hall. Three generations of the McQueston family lived here from 1852 to 1968. The home is set amidst ornamental terraced gardens while the restored interior and original books, furniture, art, toys and china offer visitors a glimpse into life in the Victorian and Edwardian eras.

At present, a public/private consortium is planning to renovate and restore Auchmar House. Located at the top of the Mountain at the corner of West 5th and Fennell, this mansion was originally built by Isaac Buchanan, a local businessman and contemporary of McNab. Amongst Buchanan's many accomplishments were the founding of both the Toronto and Hamilton Boards of Trade, the founding of the Royal Hamilton Light Infantry and the Hamilton Club. A proponent of free trade, he served as the first president of the Board of Trade for 16 years. Since 1945, his estate has been home to an order of nuns who now share it with a private health clinic.

The Hamilton Children's Museum, located in Gage Park, affords children aged 2 to 10 a multi-sensory hands-on experience and the opportunity to discover, explore and wonder about the world. Exhibits are changed twice a year and are designed to appeal to preschool, primary and junior aged children.

THE ART GALLERY OF HAMILTON IS THE THIRD LARGEST IN ONTARIO WITH OVER 8,000 PIECES OF EUROPEAN, CANADIAN AND AMERICAN ART. PHOTO BY MIKE GRANDMAISON.

WHITEHERN, HOME TO THREE GENERATIONS OF THE McQUESTON FAMILY, IS A NATIONAL HISTORIC SITE. SET AMIDST ORNAMENTAL TERRACED GARDENS, THE HOME'S COLLECTION OF ORIGINAL BOOKS, FURNITURE, ART, TOYS AND CHINA OFFERS VISITORS A GLIMPSE INTO LIFE IN THE VICTORIAN AND EDWARDIAN ERAS. PHOTO BY MIKE GRANDMAISON.

Located in the original 1859 waterworks, The Hamilton Museum of Steam and Technology showcases the technology used in the 19th century at the beginning of Canada's industrial revolution. Two Canadian made 70 ton steam engines have been preserved and are the oldest surviving examples of this type of engine left in the country. During the warmer seasons, model steam engines run on an outdoor track while the Keefer Gallery inside puts on changing exhibits and displays.

The Gallery is named for Thomas C. Keefer, a pioneering engineer who built the facility that pumped water from lake Ontario to the city. Keefer went on to build similar waterworks throughout Canada. The original steam engines operated for 51 years until they were replaced in 1910 by electric and steam turbine pumps.

The Ontario Workers' Arts and Heritage Centre is the only museum in the country dedicated to preserving the legacy of labour and working people. In 1995, the organization purchased the old Custom House in the heart of a North Hamilton working class neighborhood. The building is one of the oldest remaining federal government buildings in Canada and reflects the rise of Hamilton as a major railway city and Great Lakes port. Built between 1858-1860, it is an example of Italianate architecture and drew its inspiration from the Renaissance palaces of Rome and Florence.

The centre preserves and celebrates the arts and culture of working people and, in addition to on-site exhibits, it sends its exhibits travelling throughout the province.

LOCATED IN THE HEART OF HISTORIC DUNDAS, THE ANDREW CARNEGIE LIBRARY BUILDING HOUSES A NON-PROFIT, ARTIST-RUN GALLERY WITH EXHIBITION AREAS AND SHOPS. PHOTO BY MIKE GRANDMAISON.

THE ONTARIO WORKERS ARTS AND HERITAGE CENTRE IS THE ONLY MUSEUM IN THE COUNTRY DEDICATED TO PRESERVING THE LEGACY OF LABOUR AND WORKING PEOPLE. PHOTO BY MIKE GRANDMAISON.

Located at the airport is the Canadian Warplane Heritage Museum—Canada's finest aviation museum. It is home to 29 vintage aircraft in a state-of-the-art building. Visitors can climb into the cockpits of modern and vintage planes and, weather and crew permitting, can even go for a test flight. Traditionally held on Father's Day is the Hamilton International Air Show featuring some of the latest aircraft from around the world.

Football fans will not be able to pass up a visit to the Canadian Football Hall of Fame near City Hall and Whitehern. The permanent home of the Grey Cup, the museum houses displays on the greatest players and coaches from the Canadian Football League. Visitors can even relive some of the thrilling action from old games in the highlights films that are regularly shown.

For a taste of the turbulent history of the area, a visit to Battlefield Park in Stoney Creek is in order. The original Gage family homestead, Battlefield House, has been preserved as a museum while the 34-acre park serves as a monument to the Battle of Stoney Creek in 1813. American troops invaded from the Niagara Peninsula and after capturing Fort George in Niagara-on-the-Lake, advanced to Stoney Creek.

The British troops retreated to the Burlington Heights where Dundurn Castle later was built while the U.S. forces took over the Gage House as their headquarters. A local 19-year-old youth snuck through the American lines to warn the British that the Americans had camped in Stoney Creek. He then guided 700 regular troops under Lieutenant Colonel John Harvey through the night for a surprise attack.

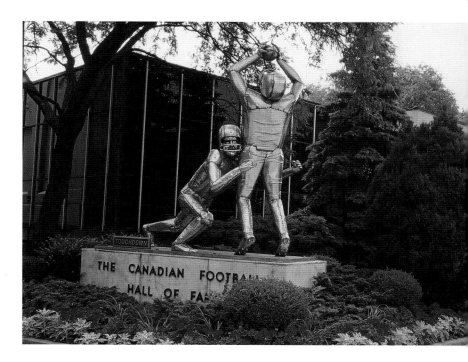

THE CANADIAN FOOTBALL HALL OF FAME IS THE PERMANENT HOME OF THE GREY CUP, AND ITS MUSEUM HOUSES DISPLAYS OF THE GREATEST PLAYERS AND COACHES FROM THE CANADIAN FOOTBALL LEAGUE. PHOTO BY MIKE GRANDMAISON.

THE INTRIGUING SCULPTURES IN THE IRVING ZUCKER SCULPTURE COURT IMPART AESTHETIC VALUE TO THE CITY WHILE SERVING AS MONUMENTS TO THREE-DIMENSIONAL ART. PHOTO BY MIKE GRANDMAISON.

For a taste of the turbulent history of the area, a visit to Battlefield Park in Stoney Creek is in order. Pictured above is the original Gage family homestead, Battlefield House, which has been preserved as a museum. Photo by Mike Grandmaison .

Hundreds died during the 40-minute battle, and the British captured the two American generals and some of their artillery. The Americans retreated. Now, every June, the Battle of Stoney Creek is re-enacted on the grounds of the original battlefield.

On a more practical note is the historic Hamilton Farmers' Market. Now located entirely indoors in Jackson Square and the Central Library, the market has been going strong since 1837. Open year-round, it provides a wide selection of seasonal fruit and vegetables, meats, cheeses, baked goods, flowers and fresh fish.

On the northern periphery of the newly expanded Hamilton is the African Lion Safari—home to more than 1,000 animals of 132 species, many of which are either endangered or threatened. Visitors can drive through the park area in their own car or on a Safari Bus and see elephants, tigers, monkeys and other exotic animals in their own environment.

Near the Safari is the Westfield Heritage Centre. This attraction sits on 39 acres of village surrounded by 324 acres of unspoiled natural woodlands and meadows with marked trails. The village is home to a fascinating array of historic restored buildings including a church, a one-room school and an inn and tea house. In August, there is a re-enactment of the U.S. Civil War, Autumn tours of the colours and a Christmas in the Country in December.

The Dundas Historical Society Museum tells the story of the early days of Dundas and presents examples of the furnishing and clothing from those pioneer days. It also has an outstanding collection of toys and dolls.

The new LIUNA Station is the completely restored and refurbished CN train station that has been turned into an 800-seat banquet hall, training and retirement centre and commercial space. The first in a number of projects to help revitalize the downtown core, it has a large park with fountain in the front. Photo by Mike Grandmaison.

DUNDURN CASTLE, ONE OF HAMILTON'S MOST RECOGNIZED LANDMARKS, IS A NATIONAL HISTORIC SITE THAT ILLUSTRATES THE LIFE AND TIMES OF SIR ALLAN NAPIER MACNAB, WHO LIVED FROM 1798-1862. PHOTO BY MIKE GRANDMAISON.

Visitors to Hamilton cannot help but notice the large number of beautiful old churches that dot almost every neighbourhood. The Cathedral of Christ the King on King Street West was built in 1933 and is an example of Gothic architecture. It has 82 Renaissance-style stained glass windows and Italian marble. The cathedral organ, one of the finest in the country, has over 4,900 pipes. Downtown on James Street South is St. Paul's Presbyterian, which was opened for prayer in March 1857. Also built in the Gothic style, it features a spire that rises 55 metres above ground level. The spire was restored in 1989 and the church was designated a provincial and national historic site.

Hamilton is also known as the "festive region" because the city is host to a different festival every month of the year. During the summer, there is a festival just about every weekend. The Festival of Friends has been held every August for over 20 years and is the largest showcase in the country for Canadian musical talent. The three day gathering in Gage Park celebrates the best in music, visual arts, crafts and food.

In July is Aquafest, a four-day waterfront festival that includes concerts, a midway, live theatre and hydroplane races. Also in July is the Hess Village Performing Arts Jazz Festival. This is a free outdoor music festival in the downtown "village" of outdoor cafes and bars. In addition to the June air show and Battle of Stoney Creek, there is the Greater Hamilton Military Tattoo featuring pipes, drums and dancers at Copps Coliseum.

BUILT IN 1933, THE CATHEDRAL OF CHRIST THE KING IS A FINE EXAMPLE OF GOTHIC ARCHITECTURE. IT HAS 82 RENAISSANCE-STYLE STAINED GLASS WINDOWS, ONE OF THE FINEST CATHEDRAL ORGANS IN THE COUNTRY, AND ITALIAN MARBLE THROUGHOUT. PHOTO BY MIKE GRANDMAISON.

Other celebrations include the Dundas Buskingfest and Cactus Festivals, Stoney Creek Flag Day, Ancaster Heritage Days, the Boris Brott Music Festival, the Winona Peach Festival, Winterfest, Oktoberfest and Festitalia, which is a month long celebration of the city's Italian inhabitants. These are just a few of the many opportunities that Hamiltonians have to go out and celebrate. ■

THE ROYAL BOTANICAL GARDENS PROVIDE A NATURAL PARADISE WITHIN THE CITY LIMITS.
PHOTOS BY MIKE GRANDMAISON.

GOING STRONG SINCE 1837, THE HISTORIC HAMILTON FARMERS' MARKET PROVIDES A VAST SELECTION OF SEASONAL FRUIT AND VEGETABLES, MEATS, CHEESES, BAKED GOODS, FLOWERS AND FRESH FISH. PHOTOS BY MIKE GRANDMAISON.

CHAPTER 5

SPORTS & OUTDOOR ACTIVITIES

Throughout Canada, Hamilton is noted
for two things: steel and the Tiger-Cats.
The familiar black and gold has long been
a mainstay of the professional Canadian
Football League and an arch rival of the
nearby Toronto Argonauts. Hamilton football
clubs have won the Grey Cup in every
decade of the 20th Century and are matched
only by the legendary Montreal Canadiens
as the winningest professional
sports team in Canada.

■ ■ ■ ■ ■ ■

THE TIGER-CATS ARE AS SYNONYMOUS WITH HAMILTON AS THE WORD "STEEL."
PHOTO BY SANDY BELL.

A FARM TEAM OF THE EDMONTON OILERS, THE HAMILTON BULLDOGS MAKE THEIR HOME AT COPPS COLISEUM. PHOTO BY SANDY BELL.

ince 1910, Hamilton teams have appeared in the Grey Cup finals 29 times and taken home the cup 15 times. Not only did the Ti-cats win the last Grey Cup of the Millennium in 1999 but they also won the Dominion championship in 1908—a year before the introduction of the Cup. Although there have been many highlights over the years, one that stands out is the infamous "Fog Bowl" played in Toronto in 1962. During the game, fog began to roll in and by the fourth quarter, it became so bad that not even the players could see each other on the field. The game was delayed with only nine minutes remaining and finished the next day. Winnipeg beat Hamilton 28/27.

The actual Tiger-Cats first appeared in 1950 but the original Hamilton Football Club was begun in 1869, just two years after Confederation and the founding of modern Canada. The team was known as the Tigers, but after World War II, a new club called the Wildcats was formed. The two amalgamated in 1950 into the team that we know today.

For exciting hockey play, there are the Hamilton Bulldogs of the American Hockey League, which make their home at Copps Coliseum. The AHL is comprised of young players waiting to make that next step into the NHL. The Bulldogs are a farm team of the Edmonton Oilers and local fans have an opportunity to watch the stars of tomorrow mature and hone their skills.

When it comes to participatory sports, Hamilton has a great deal to offer people of all ages and every interest. There are a number of baseball, basketball, curling, hockey, soccer, lacrosse, volleyball, wrestling and track and field groups throughout the area.

Thanks to the valleys and conservation areas, the region is ideal for walking, bird watching, jogging and cycling. These activities can be enjoyed alone or in the company of others. The Bruce Trail Association, the Royal Botanical Gardens and the conservation areas organize walks and hikes. The Hamilton Cycling Club has been in existence since 1889 and they have an extensive program ranging from easy rides through to time trials and races.

THE HAMILTON BULLDOGS OF THE AMERICAN HOCKEY LEAGUE MAKE THEIR HOME AT HAMILTON'S COPPS COLISEUM. THE AHL IS COMPRISED OF YOUNG PLAYERS WAITING TO MAKE THAT NEXT STEP INTO THE NATIONAL HOCKEY LEAGUE. PHOTO BY MIKE GRANDMAISON.

THE CHEDOKE CIVIC GOLF COURSE IS LOCATED IN THE WEST END OF HAMILTON AND HAS TWO 18-HOLE, PAR-70 COURSES, EACH WITH A DISTINCTIVELY DIFFERENT TERRAIN. CHEDOKE IS AMONG SOME OF THE FINEST GOLF COURSES IN SOUTHERN ONTARIO, ALL LOCATED WITHIN A SHORT DRIVE OF DOWNTOWN HAMILTON. PHOTO BY MIKE GRANDMAISON.

Hamilton, in fact, is such an ideal spot for cycling that the 2003 World Cycling Championships will be held in the city. This is one of the very few times that this prestigious race will be held outside of Europe. The race is expected to draw hundreds of thousands of tourists to the area and will be seen on worldwide television by millions of viewers. Long-distance runners can even race in an international event that has seen many of the finest runners in the world compete in Hamilton. The Around the Bay 30-km run is the oldest long distance competition in North America. It was first run on Christmas Day in 1894 and predates the Boston Marathon by three years.

For those who love the water, yachting and sailing facilities are available nearby at Pier Four and the Royal Hamilton Yacht Club on the Bay and at Fifty Point on Lake Ontario. For a slightly different form of water sport for the kids, there is the Wild Waterworks at Van Wagners Beach. This 205-acre park features Canada's largest wave pool, the Demon Slide, the Action River, tube rides and Little Squirt Works for the younger children.

And then there is golf. Some of the finest golf courses in southern Ontario are within a short drive of downtown Hamilton. In addition to some private clubs and driving ranges and mini- golf centres, there are approximately 16 public or semi-private clubs in the immediate area. The Chedoke Civic course is located in the west end of

Hamilton and has two 18-hole par 70 courses, each with a distinctly different terrain. King's Forest in the east end will provide any low handicapper with a superior challenge. Junior golfers will also find their competitive drive satisfied by competing in the Wilson Junior Golf Tour (the Hamilton/Halton Junior Championship), which was the first of its kind in Canada.

During the winter, the Chedoke course becomes the Chedoke Winter Sports Park and offers skiing on three slopes ranging in complexity from beginners to advanced. There are three T-bars and all the hills are patrolled by the Canadian Ski Patrol. Both night skiing and instruction are available and the park has full snow making and grooming facilities.

Racing fans can also enjoy world-class harness racing year round just 10 minutes from downtown at Flamborough Downs. Spectators can relax over a good meal in the fully licensed dining room on the premises. Flamborough Speedway, in contrast, affords spectators the opportunity to enjoy numerous different classes of car racing including endurance and demolition derbies. ■

FOR THOSE WHO LOVE THE WATER, YACHTING AND SAILING FACILITIES ARE AVAILABLE AT PIER FOUR
AND THE ROYAL HAMILTON YACHT CLUB ON THE BAY, AND AT FIFTY POINT ON LAKE ONTARIO.
PHOTOS BY MIKE GRANDMAISON.

HAMILTON OFFERS SPORTING OPPORTUNITIES FOR PEOPLE OF ALL AGES AND EVERY INTEREST, INCLUDING BASEBALL, BASKETBALL, CURLING, HOCKEY, SOCCER, LACROSSE, VOLLEYBALL, WRESTLING, WATER SPORTS, TRACK AND FIELD AND MORE. HAMILTON IS SUCH AN IDEAL SPOT FOR CYCLING THAT THE 2003 WORLD CYCLING CHAMPIONSHIPS WILL BE HELD IN THE CITY. LONG DISTANCE RUNNERS CAN PARTICIPATE IN THE AROUND THE BAY 30 KM RUN, WHICH IS AN INTERNATIONAL EVENT AND THE OLDEST LONG-DISTANCE COMPETITION IN NORTH AMERICA, PREDATING THE BOSTON MARATHON BY THREE YEARS. PHOTOS BY MIKE GRANDMAISON.

THANKS TO THE VALLEYS AND CONSERVATION AREAS, THE REGION IS IDEAL FOR WALKING, BIRD WATCHING, JOGGING AND CYCLING. THESE ACTIVITIES CAN BE ENJOYED ALONE OR IN THE COMPANY OF OTHERS. THE BRUCE TRAIL ASSOCIATION, THE ROYAL BOTANICAL GARDENS AND THE CONSERVATION AREAS ORGANIZE WALKS AND HIKES. PHOTO BY MIKE GRANDMAISON.

LOCAL LAKES AND STREAMS PROVIDE A RETREAT FOR PEOPLE OF ALL AGES. FOR THOSE WHO PREFER SOMETHING A LITTLE MORE WILD, THERE IS WILD WATERWORKS AT VAN WAGNERS BEACH—A 205-ACRE PARK FEATURING CANADA'S LARGEST WAVE POOL, THE DEMON SLIDE, THE ACTION RIVER, TUBE RIDES, AND LITTLE SQUIRT WORKS FOR THE YOUNGER CHILDREN. PHOTOS BY MIKE GRANDMAISON.

IN WINTER, FROZEN LAKES AND PONDS SUCH AS THIS ONE IN COOTES PARADISE BECOME A HAVEN FOR HOCKEY PLAYERS, RECREATIONAL SKATERS, AND ICE SAILORS. PHOTOS BY SANDY BELL.

THE TIGER CATS ARE A MAINSTAY OF THE PROFESSIONAL CANADIAN FOOTBALL LEAGUE, AND MANY OF ITS PLAYERS ARE HONORED IN THE CANADIAN FOOTBALL HALL OF FAME, LOCATED IN HAMILTON. HAMILTON FOOTBALL CLUBS HAVE WON THE GREY CUP IN EVERY DECADE OF THE 20TH CENTURY, AND ARE MATCHED ONLY BY THE MONTREAL CANADIENS AS THE WINNINGEST PROFESSIONAL SPORTS TEAM IN CANADA. PHOTOS BY SANDY BELL.

WHETHER IT'S RUGBY OR FOOTBALL OR ANY OTHER SPORT, COLLEGE ATHLETICS KEEP HAMILTON HOPPING WITH EXCITEMENT ALL YEAR LONG. PHOTOS BY SANDY BELL.

CHAPTER 6

SHOPPING, DINING & NIGHTLIFE

Like most cities everywhere, Hamilton has shopping malls that provide the diversity and convenience of large department stores, chains and specialty independent shops all under one roof. Regardless of what part of the city people reside in, they have easy access to Limeridge Mall, Centre Mall, Eastgate Square and Jackson Square. Ancaster is also home to the Meadowlands—an area of large "box stores" with plenty of parking.

■ ■ ■ ■ ■ ■

HAMILTON OFFERS A PERFECT MIX OF SHOPPING AND DINING POSSIBILITIES, FROM LARGE, MODERN MALLS TO QUAINT SPECIALTY SHOPS AND RESTAURANTS IN THE HEART OF THE CITY. PHOTO BY MIKE GRANDMAISON.

However, there are also areas within the city for those who just love to browse in the outdoors or who want to find an area that specializes in a particular product. The Ottawa Street area in the east end of the city is home to over 100 shops with many that specialize in textiles. Here, shoppers who are into making their own clothes can find everything they are looking for to satisfy their hobby.

Locke Street, on the western edge of the downtown core, has rapidly evolved over the past few years into the antique centre for the city. When shoppers tire of browsing through the specialty shops in the area, they can rest in one of the bars, tea shops or restaurants. A little further west and the shopper finds Westdale Village. Adjacent to McMaster University and the original shopping district for the tree-lined neighborhood of stately homes that surround it, this area has become a mix of people and shops.

Here, students, other residents, and visitors alike browse the pubs, restaurants, coffee shops, bookstore, library, unique collection of merchants or take in a movie. The focal point of the area is the historic movie house which is the last fully operational old-time neighbourhood cinema left in the city. Moving just a little farther west brings the shopper to the historic town of Dundas with its restored main street of shops, restaurants, book stores and art gallery. For Christmas family shopping, the merchants provide free sleigh rides for the children, hot apple cider and a strolling Victorian choir singing Christmas carols.

WESTDALE VILLAGE, ADJACENT TO MCMASTER UNIVERSITY, IS THE ORIGINAL SHOPPING DISTRICT FOR THE TREE-LINED NEIGHBORHOOD OF STATELY HOMES THAT SURROUND IT. TODAY, THE AREA HAS BECOME AN ECLECTIC MIX OF PEOPLE AND SHOPS THAT OFFERS A UNIQUE SHOPPING AND DINING EXPERIENCE. PHOTOS BY MIKE GRANDMAISON.

Back downtown, Gore Park and its fountain provide a centre-piece for the diverse shops, restaurants, hotels and entertainment venues. Adjacent to the main core and just to the east is the International Village. Six blocks of shops, ethnic restaurants, boutiques and the home of Theatre Aquarius.

Just north of the downtown core is the James Street North (or Jamesville) area. At the very north end is the new LIUNA Station. This is the completely restored and refurbished CN train station that has been turned into an 800-seat banquet hall, training and retirement centre and commercial space. The first in a number of projects to help revitalize the downtown core, it has a large park with a fountain in the front. There are plans as well to erect a monument to those tens of thousands of immigrants who first came by train from their ships in Halifax and got off at the Hamilton train station.

Between the station and the downtown core are numerous shops and ethnic restaurants that line James Street In the middle of the shopping area is the historic Christ Church Cathedral and the still-functioning Hamilton Armory that is home to the city's local militia units.

Thanks to the very multicultural makeup of Hamilton, there are no end of cuisines that people can try in the various ethnic establishments throughout the city. Fine dining is available from the traditional to the very exotic in a range of prices that will accommodate just about any budget. Food can also be enjoyed on the many patios, particularly in Hess Village, in the summer, in renovated historic buildings or on the waterfront.

It is a rare night that does not have live music being performed somewhere in the city. Whether it is jazz, blues, rock, country or a strolling Gypsy violinist serenading diners, there is something for just about every taste in music. ■

THANKS TO HAMILTON'S MULTI-CULTURAL MAKEUP, THERE IS NO END OF CUISINES THAT PEOPLE CAN
TRY THROUGHOUT THE CITY. ALSO A POPULAR CHOICE IS PATIO DINING DURING PLEASANT WEATHER,
PARTICULARLY IN HESS VILLAGE, WHERE CASUAL AND FINE DINING CAN BE FOUND IN HISTORIC
RENOVATED BUILDINGS OR ON THE WATERFRONT. PHOTO BY MIKE GRANDMAISON.

LOCKE STREET, ON THE WESTERN EDGE OF THE DOWNTOWN CORE, HAS RAPIDLY EVOLVED OVER THE PAST FEW YEARS INTO THE ANTIQUE CENTRE FOR THE CITY. WHEN SHOPPERS TIRE OF BROWSING THROUGH THE SPECIALTY SHOPS IN THE AREA, THEY CAN REST IN ONE OF THE BARS, TEA SHOPS OR RESTAURANTS. PHOTOS BY MIKE GRANDMAISON. BOTTOM PHOTO BY SANDY BELL.

FINE DINING IS AVAILABLE FROM THE TRADITIONAL THROUGH TO THE VERY EXOTIC, IN A RANGE OF
PRICES THAT WILL ACCOMMODATE JUST ABOUT ANY BUDGET. PHOTOS BY MIKE GRANDMAISON.

LIKE MOST CITIES EVERYWHERE, HAMILTON HAS SHOPPING MALLS THAT PROVIDE THE DIVERSITY AND CONVENINECE OF LARGE DEPARTMENT STORES, CHAINS AND SPECIALTY INDEPENDENT SHOPS ALL UNDER ONE ROOF. ADDITIONALLY, THE CITY IS HOME TO MANY "BOX STORES" THAT OFFER SPECIALIZED GOODS IN LARGE QUANTITIES OR CONVENIENTLY LOCATED IN ONE BIG STORE. PHOTOS BY MIKE GRANDMAISON.

PART TWO

PHOTO BY MIKE GRANDMAISON.

CHAPTER 7

EDUCATION

MOHAWK COLLEGE
88-89

MCMASTER UNIVERSITY
90-91

HILLFIELD-STRATHALLAN COLLEGE
92-93

PHOTO BY MIKE GRANDMAISON.

MOHAWK COLLEGE

Staff and students at Mohawk College stand with pride on the accomplishments and innovations that have been achieved by the College since its inception. Mohawk was among the first group of colleges created by the Ontario government to provide a new level of post-secondary education for students. That is, training that would offer a new vocational and applied alternative to the more theoretical universities. These colleges would educate and train young people who could then move directly into skilled and technical jobs in the labour force.

Mohawk was the first college in Ontario to provide cooperative education where students spend part of their time in class and part of their time on the job. The school is also the largest provider of apprenticeship programs in the province. Because of the diversity of programs and the school's desire to ensure that the programs are relevant, Mohawk was also one of the first colleges to implement a regular program review. More than 1,000 people from various businesses and industries act as advisors for programs, helping to ensure that students are taught skills that are in tune with the needs of industry.

Mohawk also maintains close ties with and enjoys support from both the community and industry. Strong partnerships have been developed between the college and some of the major employers in the region like steelmakers, Stelco and Dofasco. Thanks in part to these close ties, Mohawk is able to offer students some very unique and specialized programs not found elsewhere. As the result of a partnership with Toshiba, Mohawk was able to acquire a CT scanner for hands-on learning for its students in the Medical Imaging Technology Program. It is the only school in the country to have such an advanced piece of diagnostic equipment for its teaching.

The college offers five unique programs in Packaging Management Technology, Transportation Engineering Technology, Medical Imaging Technology—Ultrasonography, Instructor for Blind and Visually Impaired, and Insurance. In addition, Mohawk College is the only institution east of Alberta with a certificate program in Disability Management. This was established in partnership with the National Institute of Disability Management and Research.

Mohawk has also partnered with McMaster University. The two educational institutions offer students an opportunity to get both a four-year Bachelor of Technology degree and a diploma in engineering technology. Students spend two years at the college and two years at McMaster. Also in collaboration with McMaster, a new facility called the Mohawk-McMaster Institute for Applied Health Sciences is opening this year on the university campus.

In order to ensure that colleges are carrying out their mandate and providing quality education, the government implemented key performance indicators (KPI) to assess all the colleges in the province. These indicators look at graduate placement, employer satisfaction and student satisfaction. Mohawk is at or above the average for all colleges in each of these measures. When it comes to finding employment, 89 per cent of Mohawk graduates have jobs within six months of their graduation.

VIEW OF THE MAIN ENTRANCE OF THE FENNELL CAMPUS OF MOHAWK COLLEGE IN HAMILTON, CIRCA 1968.

Established on a 66-acre site on the Hamilton mountain beside Hillfield-Strathallan College in 1967, Mohawk's roots actually go back an additional 20 years. In 1947, the Provincial Institute of Textiles opened on the site of what is now the Wentworth Campus. This was one of the first schools in Ontario to offer specialized post-secondary training in technical fields. Ten years later, the school was restructured and became the Hamilton Institute of Technology in response to the increasing need for technical education.

Its first class of 104 pupils was given courses in textile, electrical, electronics and mechanical technology. By the end of the millennium, Mohawk has grown to 7,900 full-time students and 50,000 part-time students and has 50,000 alumni. It has a staff of approximately 700 people and an annual budget that approaches $100 million. It provides courses in the faculties of Business and Applied Arts, Health Sciences and Human Services, and Engineering Technology along with a faculty of continuing education. These faculties provide training in 70 full-time programs with an additional 1,000 programs offered on a part-time basis.

Over the past decade, funding for post-secondary education declined by 40 per cent while enrollment increased by 33 per cent. Through the efforts of the Ontario Student Opportunity Trust Fund, Mohawk was able to raise $3 million to help students in need with the cost of education. This amount was matched by the provincial government. As a result of this successful campaign, Mohawk College is able to offer significant bursaries and scholarships to more than 600 students annually.

Because the College is conscious of the need to be fiscally responsible and accountable to the public, Mohawk has developed and implemented a financial plan as part of its strategic-planning process. This is to ensure that the college balances its budget while still maintaining an appropriate level of reserves and allocation of resources. The administration plans to pursue alternative sources of revenue and develop partnerships and entrepreneurial activities within a context of cost effectiveness and accountability.

As the very name of the College was chosen to honour the original Mohawk inhabitants of this area, Mohawk continues to promote access for Aboriginal students, including the development of a new Aboriginal lounge, a brochure describing Aboriginal student services and post-secondary programs and the establishment of the Secondary School Native Advisory Committee.

Of course, a well rounded education involves more than just academics. Mohawk students have their own recreation centre that is built around the original root cellar that stored vegetables for the farm that previously occupied the area. Athletics are also a large part

MAIN ENTRANCE, FENNELL CAMPUS, TODAY.

of the school and Mohawk is quite proud of the fact that it has won more medals than any other college in Ontario.

As well, Mohawk students have their first opportunity in 2000-2001 to live on the Fennell Campus. A new four-storey residence, with an occupancy of 342, offers students a safe, social and academic environment just steps from the Student Centre, library and athletic complex. ■

McMaster University

In presenting Hamilton's McMaster University with a $10-million research and development grant to establish two leading-edge centres in health and engineering in the Fall of '99, Ontario cabinet minister Jim Wilson stated that "they would not have received these awards if they weren't absolutely the best in those areas of research." Wilson, the minister responsible for energy, science and technology in Ontario, called McMaster "a Canadian research powerhouse and worldwide leader."

The establishment of the Manufacturing Research Centre and the Centre for Gene Therapeutics is another example of what President Peter George refers to as the role the university plays in helping to diversify the economy of the region from one that is reliant solely upon heavy industry to one that also encompasses a knowledge-based industry.

LUSH, GREEN AND IDYLLIC. McMASTER UNIVERSITY IS SITUATED ON 300 ACRES BELOW THE NIAGARA ESCARPMENT AND IS BOUNDED ON THREE SIDES BY THE ROYAL BOTANICAL GARDENS AND THE COOTES PARADISE CONSERVATION AREA.

However, the university "does not turn its back on heavy industry," he said, but enhances that activity. Organizations like the new Centre for Manufacturing and the Centre for Steel Research tie back into the region's heavy industry base and help to augment their activities. In addition to creating new jobs for the region and helping to keep graduates in Hamilton, many of the university's research activities help to keep Hamilton industry up to date and competitive in the world market.

McMaster, in fact, has a long and cooperative history with the City of Hamilton. The university was originally founded and located in Toronto. It was named after its benefactor, Senator William McMaster, who was the first president of the Bank of Commerce. Originally a small Baptist liberal arts school, it was successfully wooed to Hamilton in 1930.

Enthusiastic Hamilton supporters of the school, including the city council, raised $500,000 at the beginning of the depression. To establish the Hamilton Campus, they donated a hundred acres of land in the west end near Cootes Paradise within view of the Niagara Escarpment. The adjacent land is now a conservation area, and the picturesque campus itself is home to 72 varieties of trees and shrubs.

Since it relocated to Hamilton, the university has become one of the countries foremost teaching and research institutions.

With over 3,400 employees, McMaster is the sixth-largest employer in the region, and about 75 per cent of its employees live in the region, which helps fuel the local community. In 1997, more than $300 million was spent on school operations, research and capital. That expenditure had a gross income impact of almost $600 million. In the '97-'98 fiscal year, McMaster purchased more than $11 million in goods and services from Hamilton businesses. Current construction projects for the new University Centre, the Institute for Applied Science and various renovations, total close to $80 million.

McMaster attracts people from all over the world, and its student body is comprised of people from 78 different countries. It also has 58 educational agreements with institutions in 26 countries. However, it is still a local school since more than one-third of its almost 13,000 undergraduates in '97-'98 came from Hamilton-Wentworth. Half of its 6,200 part-time and continuing education students also came from the region. More than 26,000 alumni also call the region home.

UNIVERSITY HALL, ONE OF McMASTER UNIVERSITY'S FIVE ORIGINAL BUILDINGS. THE HISTORIC BUILDINGS HAVE BEEN NAMED THE BEST GROUP OF COLLEGIATE GOTHIC STRUCTURES IN CANADA.

The school offers 141 undergraduate degrees in six faculties—humanities, business, engineering, science, social sciences and health science. The graduate school supports 38 masters and 28 doctoral programs and the health science faculty offers an MD degree. In 1998, 3,746 degrees were granted. These were 3,057 bachelor, 462 masters, 120 doctoral and 107 medical degrees. McMaster graduates excel in all fields and count among their better-known alumni: Roberta Bondar, the Canadian astronaut; The Honourable Lincoln Alexander, a former federal cabinet minister and lieutenant governor of Ontario; Ivan Reitman, the film director; and Martin Short, actor and comedian.

Among McMaster's illustrious faculty of over 1,100 academics is a co-winner of the 1994 Nobel Prize for Physics—Dr. Bertram Brockhouse. The world renowned Faculty of Health Sciences pioneered problem based learning for its medical students. This is a teaching methodology, since adapted by Harvard, among others, in which students work on patient cases in a real or simulated clinical setting.

THE HERMAN H. LEVY GALLERY, McMASTER MUSEUM OF ART, McMASTER UNIVERSITY, FEATURING FROM LEFT: PIERRE-ALBERT MARQUET *HAMBURG, A FACTORY* 1909; CLAUDE MONET *WATERLOO BRIDGE* 1903; GUSTAVE CAILLEBOTTE *LA SEINE À GENNEVILLIERS* 1878-1894; CAIMILLE PISSARRO *POMMIERS EN FLEUR* 1870. PHOTO BY ISAAC APPLEBAUM, TORONTO.

In its March 1998 issue, *Newsweek Magazine* called McMaster the granddaddy of alternative medical schools because it "changed the face of medical education in 1965 when it recognized that would-be doctors were taught the technology rather that the humanity of medicine." In order to help foster both that sense of humanity and of learning in real situations, McMaster has numerous partnerships with hospitals and affiliated institutions throughout the region.

In further demonstrating its links with the local community and industry, McMaster has established a partnership with Mohawk College to provide bachelor of technology degrees through continuing education to Mohawk graduates. Those with a three-year technology diploma and relevant work experience can obtain a McMaster degree.

McMaster is also home to the scholarly study of Bertrand Russell, the renowned British philosopher, logician, essayist and peace advocate. His archives were acquired by the library in 1968. In addition to his personal library, scholars have access to his correspondence, tapes, manuscripts and photographs. His medals and writing desk are also on display.

Due to McMaster's expertise in so many areas, it is in a perfect position to help the region of Hamilton-Wentworth achieve its economic objectives. Those objectives are to capitalize on opportunities in information technology, to expand on its strengths within the manufacturing and service industries, to support emerging markets such as biotechnology and to develop a highly trained and adaptable workforce. ■

STATE-OF-THE-ART LABORATORIES, FACILITIES AND EQUIPMENT AT McMASTER UNIVERSITY ENSURE THAT STUDENTS, FACULTY AND RESEARCHERS LEARN AND WORK WITH CUTTING-EDGE TECHNOLOGY AND RESOURCES.

HILLFIELD-STRATHALLAN COLLEGE

Continuing to build on excellence is the intent of Hillfield-Strathallan as it begins the new millennium and prepares to celebrate its 100th birthday in September 2001. In the words of Headmaster William S. Boyer, "Our goal is to continue to investigate ways to make this an optimal learning environment both for this generation of students and for the children of our current students."

HILLFIELD-STRATHALLAN COLLEGE ENCOURAGES IN-CHARGE, SELF-DIRECTED LEARNING, WHICH PROMOTES LIFE-LONG LEARNING IN ITS STUDENTS.

The learning environment, however, is not just limited to academics. The College strives also to provide its students with all round excellence in athletics and the arts, as well as to encourage their social and ethical development and to help them develop a sense of community. Students are encouraged to help with volunteer and fund raising projects in the community. The educational philosophy is best described by the College's mission statement: "To enable our students to think and act both for themselves and for the betterment of others."

The original Highfield School for Boys was founded in 1901 by John H. Collinson with the support of Lord and Lady Aberdeen. For the first 19 years, its chairman of the board was the Lieutenant Governor of Ontario Sir John S. Hendrie. In 1918, the school was largely destroyed by fire, and it was re-established as the Hillcrest School in 1920. In 1929, having outgrown its building, it moved to new quarters on Main Street West and re-opened as Hillfield School. In 1959, its name was changed to Hillfield College.

In 1923, Miss Janet Virtue and Miss Eileen Fitzgerald founded Strathallan School for Girls. In 1961, it became Strathallan College, and the following year it merged with the boys' school and became Hillfield-Strathallan College. The newly amalgamated board of governors was able to acquire the 50-acre site on Fennell Avenue West from the Ontario Government where the campus is still located.

Today the College, with an enrollment of about 1,100 students, is divided into four small schools—the Montessori school for children aged 2 1/2 to 9; primary school for ages 4 to 9; junior school for grades 5 to 8; and senior school for grades 9 to OAC.

Hillfield-Strathallan keeps current with the latest educational research and adapts its programs to provide its students with the benefit of that new knowledge. Studies have now suggested the importance of the first six years in a child's development and that learning environments are far more critical in those years than were previously believed. As a result, the College enhanced the program for its youngest pupils to enable them to stay for a full day. To accommodate this change, a new modern Montessori building was built.

An important aspect of the College's philosophy is to provide a resource-rich environment in order to give the students the opportunity to become creative problem solvers. The SWAP Centre, a concept adapted from the Science North Museum in Sudbury, is one example.

THE COLLEGE'S RESOURCE-RICH ENVIRONMENT SUPPORTS THE INTEGRATION OF INFORMATION TECHNOLOGY, WHICH IS A FUNDAMENTAL PART OF THE CURRICULUM.

This is an interactive museum where pupils can take out objects in exchange for giving something back. What the pupils give back to the museum are the results of their research on topics that they find interesting and about which they would like to learn. The role of the SWAP Centre manager is to work with the students to help them complete their research and to encourage new discovery.

The Information and Design Technology Program is another example of this creative problem solving philosophy in action. A number of senior students worked on the creation of an amphibious, carbon-fiber composite aircraft. The project took place over a few years while the participants researched and learned the necessary skills to design, test and then actually build the plane. Plans are now being developed to create an ecological resource area over the next few years that can then be related to the subject of ecology.

A well-rounded education includes academics, athletics and the arts and Hillfield-Strathallan is constantly working to improve its programs. As it was beginning to outgrow its arts facilities, College officials decided to upgrade that space. The College theatre was expanded from 240 to 400 seats and an orchestra pit was added. A new music room was also built with complete practice studios equipped with the latest in sound equipment.

The College's resource-rich environment provides a dynamic learning process that encourages Hillfield-Strathallan students to take charge of their own self-directed learning. They are given the self-sufficiency and the courage to explore new ideas and to work co-operatively with others. In addition to producing adults who can be independent and interdependent, the college's goal is to graduate students who can be creative problem solvers, risk takers and life long learners as well as good citizens, useful contributors and strong leaders.

THE COLLEGE IS A MULTI-DENOMINATIONAL, CO-EDUCATIONAL DAY SCHOOL FOR STUDENTS FROM PRIMARY KINDERGARTEN AND MONTESSORI 2½ THROUGH TO UNIVERSITY ENTRANCE.

That goal is being realized as over 98 per cent of Hillfield-Strathallan graduates go on to higher education. Alumni have made an impact in many areas of society. In politics and the law are Sir Edwin Leather, '33, the former governor of Bermuda; Justice Coulter A. Osborne, '50, of the Ontario Court of Appeal; The Honourable Colin S. Lazier, '35, a former Hamilton judge and Colin Gibson, '35, a former member of parliament.

In business there is St. Clair Balfour, '22, a publisher; Ross Dixon, '30, a local Hamilton business leader and Ron Bremner, '67, the president and CEO of the Calgary Flames Hockey Team.

In the arts there is Steve Paikin, '78, host of TVO's Studio 2; Gema Zamprogna, '92, star of Road to Avonlea; Kathleen Robertson, '92, star of Beverly Hills 90210; Martin Beaver, '85, a renowned violinist and Peter C. Newman, '47, a noted Canadian author and broadcaster. ■

HILLFIELD-STRATHALLAN COLLEGE STRIVES TO DEVELOP THE "WHOLE CHILD," WHICH INCLUDES OFFERING A WELL-BALANCED CURRICULUM OF ACADEMIC, ARTISTIC AND ATHLETIC PROGRAMS.

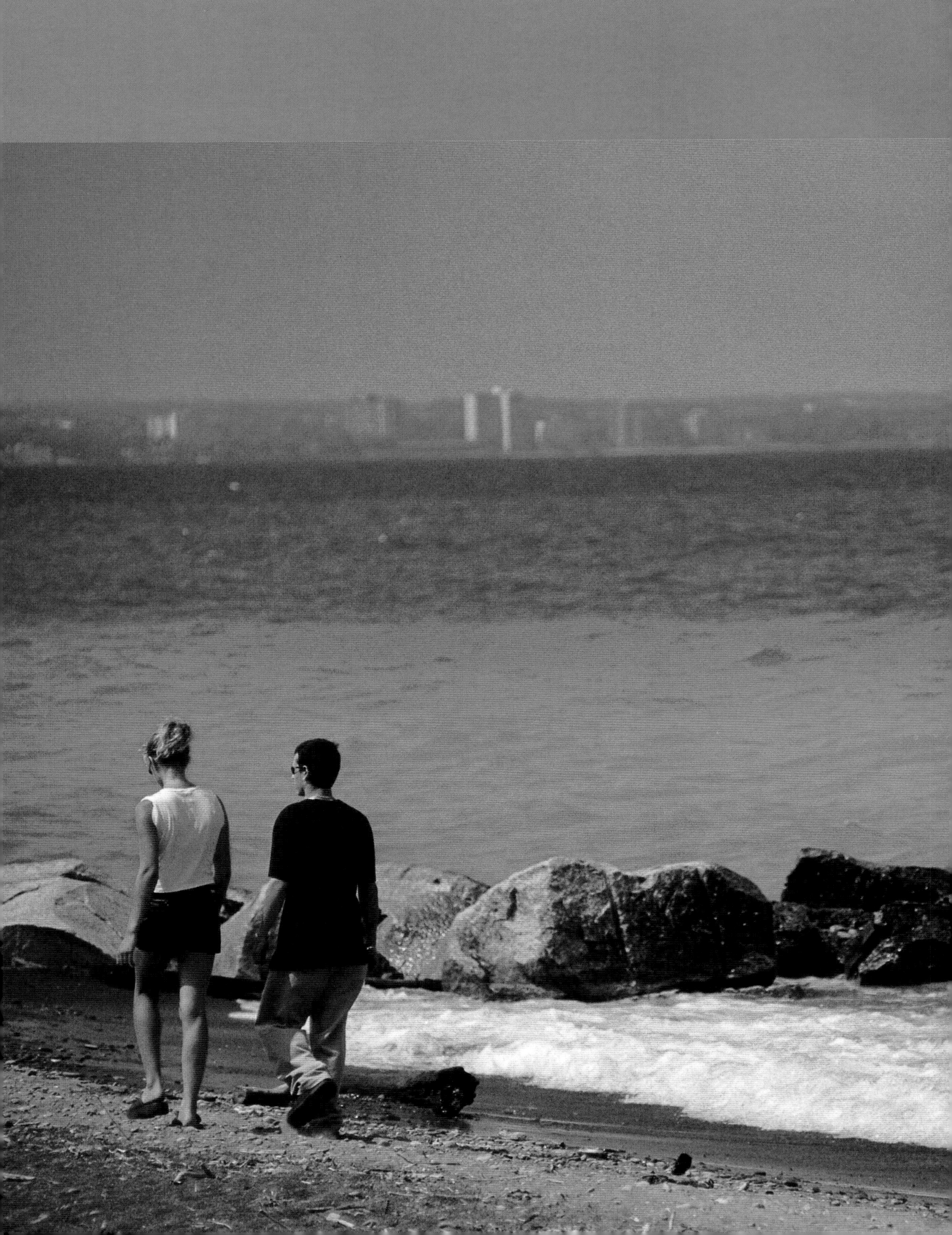

CHAPTER 8

HEALTH CARE

PHOTO BY MIKE GRANDMAISON.

HAMILTON HEALTH SCIENCES CORPORATION

Residents of Hamilton-Wentworth can pride themselves on having the largest provider of comprehensive health-care services in all of Ontario in the Hamilton Health Sciences Corporation (HHSC). This hospital also has the distinction of being the largest academic health service facility in Canada. Through its affiliation with the Faculty of Health Sciences at McMaster University, HHSC provides comprehensive care not only for Hamilton but also for the Ontario Ministry of Health's Central West Region. This encompasses the area from Niagara Falls to North of Guelph and from Oakville through to Brantford and Simcoe.

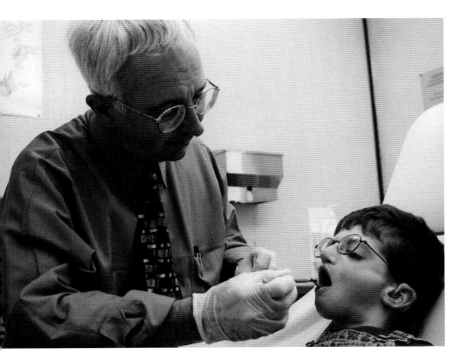

BESIDES A COMMITMENT TO CARING FOR PATIENTS, TEACHING AND RESEARCH, AN IMPORTANT PART OF THE HAMILTON HEALTH SCIENCES CORPORATIONS' MISSION IS TO HELP BUILD HEALTHY COMMUNITIES AND TO PREVENT ILLNESS BEFORE IT STRIKES.

With approximately 1,400 beds, HHSC is not physically the largest in Ontario but it is the only hospital that provides services to its patients from preconception in its Invitro Fertilization Clinic through to chronic and palliative care. The hospital has four locations throughout the city. The Hamilton General is in the eastern part of downtown, the Henderson General is on the east mountain, while Chedoke is on the west mountain and McMaster University Medical Centre (which includes the Children's Hospital) is in the west end and part of the campus of McMaster University. These four locations provide comprehensive services to all age groups and for all medical conditions.

The very creation of the HHSC just a few years ago was a progressive, proactive and unusual merger that demonstrated the commitment of Hamilton's citizens to forging partnerships and collaborations to enhance health care. HHSC is an amalgamation of the former Hamilton Civic Hospitals (Hamilton and Henderson Generals) with Chedoke-McMaster. The Boards of Governors of both institutions, comprised of community volunteers, realized that money could be saved and services improved through an amalgamation of their two institutions.

They had the foresight to predict what was going to come about in the future by the cost conscious Ontario Government. By voluntarily developing an agreed upon amalgamation plan and implementing it, they were able to avoid the strife caused by many of the forced amalgamations imposed on communities by the government. Hamilton was

able to achieve this amalgamation without the controversy that other communities in Ontario went through because the citizens already had a rich history of this type of money saving cooperation.

Because of its size and scope, HHSC can advocate on behalf of some of the smaller facilities and health and social service organizations in the region, working together in partnership to create a seamless system of care for the community. The organization is also investigating ways that some of its clinical services can be centralized to provide improved and more cost-effective medical services for the entire region. Specialty services like heart and neurosurgery, trauma, pediatrics and oncology are now being provided by HHSC for the region as these services are difficult for small community hospitals to support.

Because of its affiliation with the Faculty of Health Sciences at McMaster, HHSC also has a strong focus on teaching and research. This partnership with the medical school has enabled HHSC to attract some of the best and most innovative health-care professionals in the world. One of these physicians is Dr. Salim Yusuf, a cardiologist who came to Hamilton from the prestigious National Institute of Health in Washington. Another is Dr. Jack Hirsh who is a leader in research on blood clotting, a major cause of heart attacks and strokes.

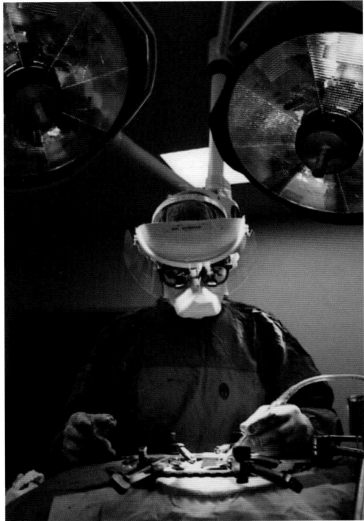

HHSC's WORLD-RENOWNED STAFF INCLUDES DR. SALIM YUSUF, CARDIOLOGIST, AND DR. JACK HIRSH, LEADER IN RESEARCH ON BLOOD CLOTTING. THE HOSPITAL OFFERS THE HAMILTON COMMUNITY OUTSTANDING SERVICE WITH SUCH TALENTED AND INNOVATIVE HEALTH-CARE PROFESSIONALS ON STAFF. PHOTO BY PHILL SNEL.

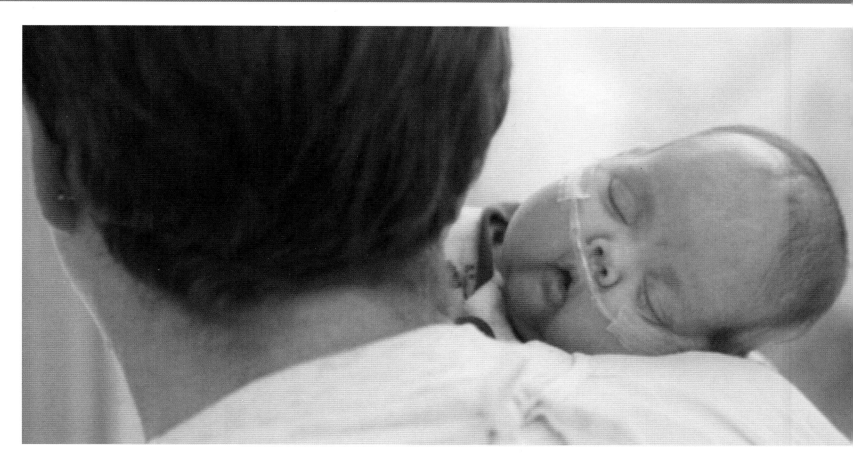

HHSC IS THE ONLY HOSPITAL IN ONTARIO TO PROVIDE COMPLETE SERVICES TO PATIENTS THROUGHOUT THEIR ENTIRE LIFE, FROM PRECONCEPTION TO CHRONIC AND PALLIATIVE CARE.

Because of the expertise and reputation of HHSC staff, they are consulted on many of the trials for new drugs that are being investigated around the world. In fact, many of those international drug trials that are evaluating the safety and suitability of new drugs are conducted at HHSC. Patients in Hamilton, who wish to, can help to test these new drugs and to benefit from those that are effective.

This research component also helps to provide a second economic focus for the region in addition to the traditional manufacturing. HHSC is the largest employer in Hamilton-Wentworth with 8,200 staff and an additional 1,000 medical personnel. The economic spin-offs from their activities and salaries in the local housing, retail and entertainment markets are considerable. Their presence and spending helps to provide countless new jobs for others.

In addition, the world-renowned staff who practice and conduct research at HHSC are attracting millions of dollars in new investment money for the region. Money to expand these research efforts (which includes the hiring of more researchers and support staff and the purchase of equipment and supplies) has come from the Medical Research Council of Canada, the Heart and Stroke Foundation and the National Cancer Institute as well as other funding bodies nationally and internationally.

Caring for patients, teaching and research are the first three elements in the hospital's mission but there is a fourth element. That is to help build healthy communities and to prevent illness before it strikes. Health promotion through partnerships with health and social agencies is an important part of HHSC's activities. Hospital staff meets on a regular basis with their counterparts in community agencies that deal with health issues. These forums allow staff from both the hospital and the agencies to become aware of new issues that might effect them and to share strategies. ■

St. Peter's Health System

The year 2000 marks a significant milestone for St. Peter's—the celebration of 110 years of service, as well as the launch of a new look, vision and mandate for the future.

Since its inception in 1890, St. Peter's has been responding to the needs of seniors and the chronically ill.

Founded by the Reverend Thomas Geoghegan, pastor of St. Peter's Anglican Church, St. Peter's was initially opened as a home for people who required chronic care—a level of care not available in the acute-care hospitals at the time. Through contributions made by citizens of the community, Reverend Geoghegan purchased the Springer mansion, which sat on the site occupied by the current building, and converted it to a 14-bed facility for those with incurable illnesses. In 1931, St. Peter's was formally recognized as a hospital under the Public Hospitals Act. Forty years later, the Hamilton District Hospital Council recommended that only chronically ill seniors be cared for at St. Peter's.

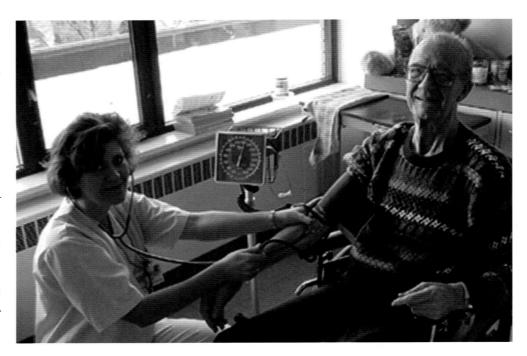

As St. Peter's community has grown in size and complexity, so have the health-care needs of its members. St. Peter's has responded to these changes by evolving into the new St. Peter's Health System. What has not changed is the unwritten but well-respected covenant of care between the community and St. Peter's that has existed for over a century.

THE YEAR 2000 MARKS A SIGNIFICANT MILESTONE FOR ST. PETER'S: THE CELEBRATION OF ITS 110TH YEAR OF SERVICE, AS WELL AS THE LAUNCH OF A NEW LOOK, VISION AND MANDATE FOR ITS FUTURE.

In 1998, as a result of provincial health care restructuring, St. Peter's was directed to close as a chronic-care hospital and, instead, explore other opportunities to provide health-care services for seniors. In an effort to ensure that seniors would continue to receive the health care they deserved, St. Peter's, together with its health-care partners and the Regional Municipality of Hamilton-Wentworth, developed a model of an integrated system of care for seniors that would also preserve St. Peter's 110-year tradition of caring.

This model positioned St. Peter's to assume management responsibility of the complex continuing-care services for the Hamilton Health Sciences Corporation and St. Joseph's Hospital, and the region's two homes for the aged; become a provider of long-term-care services; and establish a seniors' health research institute in partnership with the Faculty of Health Sciences at McMaster University.

Over the past few years, St. Peter's has been busy building this integrated system of care for seniors, and has expanded its mandate to include the chronically ill. This integrated system of care for seniors and the chronically ill is the first of its kind in the province.

Today, St. Peter's provides inpatient, community-based and outpatient services, and is responsible for the management of complex continuing-care services for the Hamilton Health Sciences Corporation and St. Joseph's Hospital. Most recently, St. Peter's expanded its mandate to include the provision of home health-care services. Under the guidance of St. Peter's, wecare Home Health Services will continue to provide individuals with the home-care services that they need and deserve.

ST. PETER'S IS LOOKING FORWARD TO THE OPPORTUNITIES THAT LIE AHEAD IN THE YEARS TO COME AS THE LEADER IN PROVIDING A CONTINUUM OF SERVICE FOR SENIORS AND CARE FOR THE CHRONICALLY ILL. THIS NEW INTEGRATED SYSTEM OF CARE WILL ENSURE THAT SENIORS AND THE CHRONICALLY ILL CONTINUE TO RECEIVE THE BEST POSSIBLE CARE AND THAT ST. PETER'S 110 YEARS OF EXPERTISE WILL CONTINUE TO IMPROVE THEIR QUALITY OF LIFE.

In addition, St. Peter's Foundation has committed $1-million to the creation of a Chair in Aging within the Faculty of Health Sciences at McMaster University. This individual will oversee important teaching and research projects that have a direct impact on the quality of life for older adults.

PRESENTLY, ST. PETER'S PROVIDES INPATIENT PROGRAMS, COMMUNITY-BASED AND OUTPATIENT SERVICES, AND IS RESPONSIBLE FOR THE MANAGEMENT OF COMPLEX CONTINUING-CARE SERVICES FOR THE HAMILTON HEALTH SCIENCES CORPORATION AND ST. JOSEPH'S HOSPITAL.

Eventually, St. Peter's Health System will become the region's largest provider of services for the elderly and care for the chronically ill. It will consist of: hospital-based complex continuing-care services, long-term-care services, home health-care services that will enable seniors to remain in their own homes longer, and retirement facilities for seniors who are unable to remain in their own homes, but do not require a hospital-type setting.

The guiding principles of integrity, respect, excellence and growth that have been such an important part of St. Peter's past achievements continue to play an important role in its growth. St. Peter's has worked hard to earn the trust of citizens and values its reputation as a company built on integrity. St. Peter's believes that all patients and family members, staff, volunteers, community partners and other individuals deserve to be treated with respect, dignity and compassion. St. Peter's is committed to achieving excellence in service, and learning and sharing knowledge with others. Finally, in an effort to keep reaching out to the community, St. Peter's is committed to growth and finding innovative ways to meet the needs of seniors and the chronically ill.

The new St. Peter's Health System will ensure that seniors and the chronically ill continue to receive the best possible care and that the 110-years of expertise accumulated by St. Peter's will continue to improve their quality of life. St. Peter's looks forward to the challenges and opportunities that lie ahead in the years to come as the region's leader in providing a continuum of service for seniors and care for the chronically ill.

Vision

To be the leader in providing a continuum of service for seniors and care for the chronically ill.

Mission

To excel at innovative client-focused service, delivered by a committed team of people through the integration of clinical, academic and administrative expertise. ■

ST. PETER'S BELIEVES THAT ALL PATIENTS AND FAMILY MEMBERS, STAFF, VOLUNTEERS, COMMUNITY PARTNERS AND OTHER INDIVIDUALS DESERVE TO BE TREATED WITH RESPECT, DIGNITY AND COMPASSION.

St. Joseph's Hospital

Founded in 1890, St. Joseph's Hospital is the largest facility of the St. Joseph's Health Care System—one of the largest corporations devoted to comprehensive health care in Canada. The range of services offered by the hospital is based on the original healing mission of the founding Sisters of St. Joseph of Hamilton and reflects the hospital's belief that it is "an honour to serve the sick, the disadvantaged, and the marginalized in our society with the very best in hospital care possible."

Along with its primary role of caring for the sick, St. Joseph's stresses the importance of teaching and research through its affiliation with McMaster University and its own Father Sean O'Sullivan Research Centre. In the past year alone, $12 million in new research money was invested in research. Spin offs from those grants help provide new jobs for the community.

St. Joseph's downtown emergency department, along with the urgent care centre at the Community Health Centre in the east end, treats over 100,000 people a year and is the busiest emergency program in the city. With over 4,000 births a year, the hospital has one of the most productive maternity wards in Ontario. In addition to having one of the largest dialysis units in the Province, St. Joseph's performs 20 per cent of all Ontario's kidney transplants.

Its 14 operating rooms make it one of the most intense surgical centres in Canada. The newly established Centre for Minimal Access

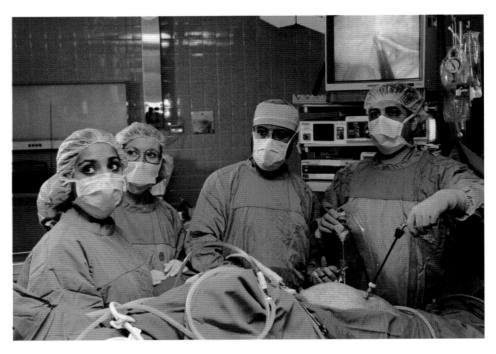

ST. JOSEPH'S HOSPITAL AND McMASTER UNIVERSITY HAVE TOGETHER CREATED AN INTERNATIONAL CENTRE FOR TEACHING SURGICAL TECHNIQUES IN THE FAST-GROWING AREA OF MINIMALLY INVASIVE THERAPY.

Surgery is the first in Canada and will use state-of-the-art technology to train surgeons and students in the techniques of "key-hole" surgery. Thanks to these new methods, patients will recover much faster and spend far less time in hospital.

The Firestone Institute for Respiratory Health has a world-class reputation for its work. More than 20,000 patients visit the Institute annually for assessment and follow up for asthma, emphysema, allergies and other respiratory problems. With its leading-edge research and the expansion of its facilities thanks to $17 million in grants, it will rank among the top three respirology facilities in the world.

Because of St. Joseph's belief in the continuum of care, the hospital is committed to providing services to people where they need it, when they need it. St. Joseph's Community Health Centre provides care in the previously under-serviced east end. Aside from physicians' offices and urgent care, there is an entire range of educational and preventative programs available along with pastoral care and the highly innovative Dr. Bob Kemp Hospice.

People suffering from severe chronic mental illnesses are assisted by the hospital through outreach and partnerships with other agencies like the nationally acclaimed Crisis Outreach and Support Team (COAST). This group of specially trained police officers, working with health-care staff, assist those in crisis in the community receive medical attention in the St. Joseph's Emergency Psychiatric Treatment Unit or other centres. ◾

A NURSE REVIEWS BABY'S FIRST PASSPORT BEFORE THE NEW MOM AND BABY ARE DISCHARGED HOME.

ST. JOSEPH'S VILLA

St. Joseph's Villa is a key member of St. Joseph's Health Care System. Founded by the Sisters of St. Joseph of Hamilton in 1879 as the House of Providence, the Villa has grown to become a recognized leader throughout Canada for its comprehensive care of the elderly.

In 1999, St. Joe's became the first long-term-care facility in North America to be awarded the ISO 9002 certification. This international designation is given to organizations that can meet very strict quality guidelines and ensures that residents receive the very best of care. The Villa was also the recipient of two national awards that year. The Honourable Hilary Weston, Lieutenant Governor of Ontario, presented St. Joseph's Villa with the Donner Canadian Foundation Award for Excellence in the Delivery of Social Services. St. Joseph's was ranked highest among 382 applicants. This award is given in conjunction with the Fraser Institute in Vancouver. The Villa also received the Donner Award for Services to Seniors recognizing its work in respite care, palliative care and outreach services.

The Government of Ontario also recognized the excellence of Villa programs when the Villa became the first long-term-care facility, out of 200 applicants, to obtain approval for its new building program.

The Villa provides care for 378 residents. It uses strong links with the community to provide assistance for those living at home. In partnership with the local Rotary Club, the Villa operates a respite-care program for seniors. When family members need a break, they simply bring their elderly relative in for a short stay. This gives the elderly a vacation as well since they can enjoy the many services and programs of the Villa.

There is an active day program for nearly 200 seniors from the community allowing others to benefit from the programs. In 1996, St. Joseph's Estates was opened. It is home to 193 seniors who live independently. The seniors have easy access to all the facilities of the Villa like the therapeutic pool and the bowling alley. When they require care, they simply move into the main building. This is ideal for couples. If one needs to move into the Villa, they are only a two-minute walk from the estates so the couple can keep in constant contact.

The Villa specializes in care and research for Alzheimer's Disease. With its on-site researcher, St. Joseph's is part of the Father Sean O'Sullivan Research Centre. Together they are able to develop leading-edge research that will help to make a difference to the lives of seniors now and in the future.

ST. JOSEPH'S VILLA PROVIDES A VIBRANT ACTIVITY CENTRE FOR NEARLY 200 SENIORS WHO PARTICIPATE IN ITS SENIORS' DAY PROGRAM ON A WEEKLY BASIS.

The residents of St. Joe's have been supported by the Hamilton community for the whole of its 120-year history. Volunteers have donated their time, expertise and money to improve life for seniors. Financial support was formalized in 1978 with the creation of St. Joseph's Villa Foundation as the fundraising arm of the Villa. Residents' quality of life is enhanced as a result of donations used to improve the living environment, pay for trips to a park, to a ball game or for just a tour around town.

The Foundation is currently involved in a Capital Fundraising Campaign to completely rebuild and renovate the Villa. The new facility will consist of Resident Home Areas which will feature increased private and semi-private rooms, private washrooms, living rooms, dens, dining rooms and an area for prayer and meditation. St. Joseph's Villa will stand as a model long-term-care facility well into the 21st Century. ■

ST. JOSEPH'S VILLA IS CENTRALLY LOCATED IN THE HEART OF DUNDAS. IT IS SURROUNDED BY BEAUTIFUL GARDENS AND FORESTS.

CHAPTER 9

MANUFACTURING

PHOTO BY MIKE GRANDMAISON.

TUBE-MAC® INDUSTRIES

What began in 1977 as a pipe repair and installation business operating out of the back of the founder Gary Mackay's pick-up truck, is today a successful North American company. From its head office in Stoney Creek, Ontario, and its offices in the United States and the United Kingdom, Tube-Mac® Industries (TMI®) provides cost-effective, environmentally friendly non-welded piping systems for clients all over the world.

Operating on quality assurances designed to meet ISO 9001, Tube-Mac® designs, manufactures and supplies non-welded piping systems for hydraulic lines, lubrication and grease lines, and paint and ink lines. Applications include sugar mills, aluminum mills, automotive simulation equipment, steel mill equipment, pulp mill equipment and log handling decks to name just a few. Tube-Mac® has been involved with projects in Canada, the United States, Central America, South America, Australia and South East Asia.

What is unique about Tube-Mac® is that it uses a non-welded system. Traditionally, pipes have been connected by welding them together. By using non-welded connections, Tube-Mac® eliminates the need for this. The advantages gained by Tube-Mac® are not only the saving of time and labour costs but also the elimination of the flushing process that is required to rid the pipe of the contamination caused by the welding. A toxic acid solution is required for the flushing process, and since the acid solution can only be used once, the solution must then be disposed of with due consideration for all of the environmental concerns. Tube-Mac's® non-welded system avoids this step entirely. In comparison, a simple oil flush removes loose particles to achieve ISO cleanliness levels after a Tube-Mac® installation. Tube-Mac's® custom designed and built flushing and pressure testing equipment can accomplish this.

TWO CENTRAL WAREHOUSES WITH COMBINED INVENTORY OF OVER 1,000 TONS OF PIPE: STONEY CREEK, ONTARIO, CANADA, AND ZELIENOPLE, PENNSYLVANIA, USA.

Depending upon the application, Tube-Mac® uses one of four types of non-welded methods to join components. These methods are flared flange, retain ring, mechanical grooved and crimp coupling. The most common method is the flare flanged system. The flared flange system is used for medium to high pressure projects and is based on flaring the pipe ends to 37 degrees. The retain ring system is typically used for higher flows with high pressures. This system uses a heavy wall pipe with a machined face, an annular groove and a retain ring which keeps the flange in position. The third method is used for low pressure hydraulic return lines or lubrication lines. A roll forming groove is made in the ends of the pipe and then a coupling with a gasket completes the joint. The final method is a non-welded crimp coupling, which is slid over the ends of the two pipes and then permanently crimped in place to form the connection.

Amy Woy, a project engineer at Republic Engineered Steel, is a satisfied customer of Tube-Mac®. Woy pointed out that the costs for the flared and retain ring non-welded systems are marginally higher than a traditional welded pipe system. "However, when the material and labour costs were analyzed and combined to identify the total installed system cost, savings were realized. Total installation cost savings far outweighed material costs."

Tube-Mac® continually explores and develops new ideas through technology and the latest manufacturing processes. Tube-Mac® designers use the latest version of AutoCAD to design piping systems and components. The in-house machine shop uses the latest

PREFABRICATED 4 INCH BROWN STOCK TOWER PERIMETER PIPING FOR THE PULP AND PAPER INDUSTRY. FINAL INSPECTION OF SHOP PREFABRICATION BEFORE DISMANTLING AND SHIPPING TO THE CUSTOMER.

CNC lathes and machining centers to manufacture standard components, custom blocks and fittings to meet customer needs.

TUBE-MAC'S 50,000-SQUARE-FOOT HEAD OFFICE LOCATED IN STONEY CREEK, ONTARIO.

Its extensive inventories in Canada and the U.S. allow Tube-Mac® to deliver products to its customers in a timely manner. This combined with the availability of TMI® Field Technicians and portable installation equipment enables Tube-Mac® to respond quickly to the needs of its customers.

TMI® piping systems are either custom fitted in the field under the direct supervision of Tube-Mac® Field Technicians or are 100 percent prefabricated in its state-of-the-art plant. Customers can e-mail their plant equipment layout drawings to Tube-Mac® designers who will superimpose the piping over these drawings. Once the client approves the system, the piping is fabricated. All components are then shipped to the customer, and the on-site Tube-Mac® Field Technician ensures that the installation is properly completed.

Tube-Mac® has the ability to provide complete turnkey responsibility for the installation including system flushing to the required ISO cleanliness level. Tube-Mac® assures that its combination of quality people, quality service and quality products will result in successful projects throughout the world.

The success Tube-Mac® has enjoyed over the years has enabled the company and its employees to take an active role in a variety of community affairs. Tube-Mac® is a corporate sponsor of the AHL Hamilton Bulldogs hockey team and also sponsors numerous minor league teams throughout the Hamilton region. Tube-Mac® is an active donor to the local Salvation Army as well as various community projects and is also a recipient of "The Canadian Red Cross" certificate of appreciation.

With a view to the future Tube-Mac® values its customers, employees and local suppliers within the Hamilton-Wentworth regional community. ■

DOFASCO

ofasco is entering the new millennium with a great deal of optimism and a greater competitive strength than at any time in its history thanks to its innovative approach of producing value-added steel products designed to solve the needs of its customers. In the past decade, over $2 billion has been invested in new technology and facilities in Hamilton, and productivity has increased over 50 per cent. That increase in productivity is double the average for the Canadian manufacturing sector. Fifty per cent of its current products were not even available 10 years ago. After a long hiatus, the company is back into hiring new staff while continuing to emphasize that "Hamilton is home" and has been since 1912.

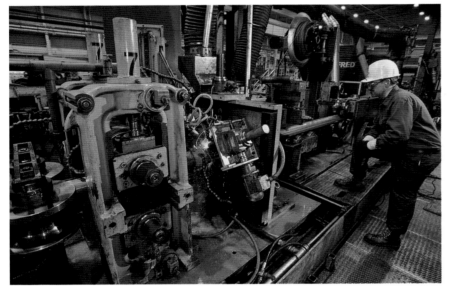

DOFASCO LEVERAGED ITS EXPERTISE IN ADVANCED METALLURGY BY BUILDING TWO MILLS IN HAMILTON TO PRODUCE LARGE-DIAMETER STEEL TUBING SPECIFICALLY FOR HYDROFORMED AUTOMOTIVE APPLICATIONS. THESE ONE-PIECE PARTS, FORMED UNDER INTENSE WATER PRESSURE, ARE LIGHTER, MORE RELIABLE, SAFER AND LESS EXPENSIVE TO MANUFACTURE. DOFASCO'S NUMBER ONE TUBE MILL IS NOW OPERATING AT FULL CAPACITY AND NUMBER TWO STARTED UP IN JUNE 2000.

Dofasco produces high quality flat rolled and tubular steel and is Canada's only producer of tinplate. Its single largest market is the automotive industry but other markets are in construction, energy, manufacturing, pipe and tube, appliance, packaging and steel distribution industries. Towards the end of 1999, Dofasco began producing a new galvanized steel product in Hamilton in partnership with Sollac of France. DoSol Galva combines the knowledge of these two steel companies in a state-of-the-art facility that produces a corrosion-resistant hot-dipped galvanized steel. This product is used primarily in exposed auto body panels.

Another innovation recently introduced by Dofasco is manufacturing tubular steel products for use in the hydroforming method producing automobile frames and chassis. A desired shape for tubing can be created by forcing water under very high pressure into them. This new methodology has resulted in a major breakthrough for the automobile industry. One single tube can now replace 15 or more welded parts. This has reduced both the cost of production and the weight of cars while increasing their safety and fuel efficiency. Dofasco scientists are now studying methods for using this technology to create one single car frame.

Another new venture for Dofasco is to share its intellectual discoveries in partnership with other companies. Dofasco has long been recognized as a leader in preventative maintenance practices and has had requests

from companies all over the world who want to acquire that system. Dofasco joined with a local maintenance software firm (Ivara) and is working with various manufacturers to implement these Hamilton solutions in plants throughout the world.

In 1999, Ivara received two of the four awards for excellence presented by the Maintenance Management Conference of Canada. The Dofasco methods received an award for the best use of technology in plant maintenance and the award for the best maintenance in a large plant.

These innovations, however, are part of the "Dofasco way." In the 1950s, the company pioneered the use of the basic oxygen furnace, which, today, still remains as the common standard for steelmaking around the world. In 1996, Dofasco fired up an electric arc furnace and slab caster, the first of its kind in North America for any fully integrated steel maker.

Since its beginning, Dofasco has taken its community responsibility very seriously. In 1997, it became the first Canadian company to sign a voluntary Environment Management Agreement with the federal and provincial governments. Dofasco committed itself to exceeding the required improvements in emissions. In the last decade, Dofasco has reduced greenhouse gases by 27 per cent. Benzene emissions are down 50 per cent since 1993, and energy use per ton has dropped by 21 per cent. Since 1995, carbon dioxide emissions have gone down 16 per cent while Canadian industry generated a 16 per cent increase. Electricity consumption has declined by 20 per cent per ton of steel produced.

The firm also plays a leadership role in the Hamilton Industrial Environmental Association—a group that includes most major companies and citizens groups. The organization's purpose is to create an integrated approach to environmental protection. Major improvements have been made to

DOFASCO PEOPLE WORK CLOSELY WITH CUSTOMERS TO DELIVER SOLUTIONS IN STEEL™, A MARKET STRATEGY DESIGNED TO DIFFERENTIATE DOFASCO AMONG STEELMAKERS. THIS MARKET STRATEGY FOCUSES ON THE NEEDS OF DOFASCO'S CUSTOMERS, BY MAKING PRODUCTS THAT HELP THEM SUCCEED WITH THEIR CUSTOMERS.

DOFASCO'S SOLUTIONS IN STEEL™ MARKET STRATEGY IS BACKED BY GROWTH STRATEGY THAT INVESTS IN INNOVATION. IN THE 1990S, DOFASCO HAS INVESTED MORE THAN CDN$2 BILLION IN NEW TECHNOLOGY AND FACILITIES.

Hamilton Harbour. Dofasco employs an almost totally closed system for its water use. Because of its environmental precautions, Dofasco has won international awards for its efforts.

Dofasco is also a major contributor to the economy of Hamilton and to the revitalization of the city. The company pays over $30 million in municipal taxes and provides over one half billion dollars in direct wages to its employees. An additional one half billion dollars is spent on goods and services in the community. But this is not all the contribution that Dofasco makes to the well being of Hamilton.

Since 1995, corporate charitable donations have exceeded $8 million plus the amount that its employees contribute through an employee fund. The company has contributed to capital campaigns of regional hospitals in addition to contributing $1 million for the purchase of another MRI for the citizens. A considerable amount is also donated to universities.

Dofasco has invested over $2 million to endow chairs in metallurgical engineering and process automation and information technology at McMaster University. This investment in education helps to develop a knowledge base in Hamilton that can be used to improve upon the local manufacturing processes and to increase business. This also results in the creation of new jobs in Hamilton for the graduates of those programs and helps to keep this talent pool in the city.

The energy, skills and talent of Dofasco staff also contribute to the well being of Hamilton. Employees donate their time and expertise to the boards of institutions like the Art Gallery of Hamilton, the United Way, the Chamber of Commerce, food banks, women's shelters and most other charitable and self help groups. If they aren't on the boards, then Dofasco employees are donating their time to help out with various volunteer functions in those organizations. ■

DOFASCO'S DOSOL GALVA FACILITY, AN 80:20 JOINT VENTURE WITH THE USINOR AUTO DIVISION OF SOLLAC OF FRANCE, UTILIZES USINOR'S WOLD-CLASS GALVANIZING TECHNOLOGY TO PRODUCE EXTRAGAL™, A CORROSION-RESISTANT, GALVANIZED STEEL FOR EXPOSED AUTO BODY PANELS. THE 450,000-TONS-PER-YEAR DSG FACILITY IS LOCATED AT DOFASCO'S HAMILTON OPERATIONS, IN HAMILTON, ONTARIO.

AMCAN CASTINGS LIMITED

As AMCAN Castings Limited continues its production into the new millennium from its beginnings in the Great Depression, it offers ample proof of the benefits that can be derived for both the company and its employees from using the new technology and robotics. The company, which designs and manufactures high pressure aluminum die cast parts for the automotive industry, has increased its sales from $20 million per year in 1992 to a projected $240 million in 2000. This increase in productivity through automation was completed with no reduction in its workforce, with the help of its workers and with no labour disputes. Along the way, it won community awards for its business excellence and its contributions to the community.

AMCAN first began operation in Hamilton as Barber Die Casting in 1936. In 1942, it moved to its present site on Hillyard Street in the North End, and, in 1945, its employees joined the United Steel Workers Union as local 4153. As proof of its excellent labour relations record, it points to the fact that the company has never had a strike.

Barber Die changed its name to AMCAN in 1982 and it is now the largest division of AMCAN Consolidated Technolgies. In addition to a location in Burlington, AMCAN owns the largest die cast company in Brazil and will soon be expanding into Mexico. Other sites are in Europe and Renfrew, Ontario.

AMCAN CASTINGS LIMITED NEW CORPORATE OFFICES AND TECHNOLOGY CENTRE, HAMILTON, ONTARIO.

AMCAN designs, tests and casts automobile body, engine, drive train and steering and suspension components as well as various power steering brackets and air conditioner brackets for all the major car manufacturers. Over 17 million components were made for GM, Ford, Chrysler and their suppliers in 1998 and close to 50 million components are projected for 2001. All the four-by-four differential carriers, oil pans and front end brackets for Chrysler and all the differential carriers and transfer cases for GM four by fours are done in Hamilton by AMCAN. Oil pans are made for Ford Escorts/Focus and various Chrysler models.

AMCAN officials like to remind themselves and their workers that they are making parts for cars that their friends and families are likely to own and drive. Constantly reminding themselves of their involvement with a finished product gives AMCAN management and staff a greater appreciation for the need to ensure safe high-quality components.

AMCAN engineers, working with their customers, use state-of-the-art computer software to design, simulate and test all components. The computer analysis tells the design engineers where components are weak and might break so that modifications can be made prior to manufacture or that different alloys might be required. As a result of this simulation, productivity has increased by 10 per cent and wastage has declined by 10 per cent.

Computer studies did demonstrate that magnesium would be a much better metal than aluminum for instrument panels. In a crash, magnesium bends with the impact unlike aluminum that snaps off and can impale the driver. Switching to magnesium helps to save lives and reduce the severity of injuries.

Starting in 1998, AMCAN's Trimag Division started supplying GM with a magnesium steering column support beam resulting in a weight reduction of eight pounds. The switch to magnesium also meant that the assembly was reduced from seven stamped weldments to just one precision-machined Magnesium die-casting.

As the result of AMCAN's development of the front-end accessory drive brackets for the Ford 5.0L Explorer, the company won Ford's Outstanding Achievement in Engineering Award. AMCAN was able to complete two full bracket designs and deliver die cast production parts to Ford only eight months after the idea was first proposed.

AUTOMATED PRODUCTION LINE (EXTRACTION PROCESS) USING STATE-OF-THE-ART ROBOTICS.

4,000-TON IDRA PRESSE—ONE OF THE LARGEST DIE CAST MACHINES IN NORTH AMERICA.

In addition, AMCAN was able to optimize the die casting process, improve the performance and functionality and reduce system cost and complexity for the Ford Ranger series bracket design. AMCAN engineers were able to eliminate a total of four stamped parts and six fasteners thus reducing the weight by 3.7 pounds.

AMCAN's Hamilton location employs about 400 people in a 110,000-square-foot facility with 26 die casting machines. The machines range in size from 600 tons to 4,000 tons and cast components range in size from as small as 1.0 to over 60 pounds. The Hillyard Avenue site in Hamilton has just been expanded with AMCAN investing over $50 million in improvements. With the help of its employees, production continued at its normal pace while staff worked under cover of tarpaulins during one stage of the expansion.

Because of its desire to be a good corporate neighbour, AMCAN spent a significant portion of the money for expansion in fixing up the exterior of its building and improving the landscape. By keeping its neighbours informed of its plans, AMCAN acted as a catalyst for others in the area to improve their properties as well. In 1999, AMCAN was presented with the Trillium Award from the Region of Hamilton-Wentworth for its efforts to beautify and improve the area.

In 1997, the company was presented with the Hamilton and District Chamber of Commerce Big Business Award to recognize its outstanding achievements in business within Hamilton-Wentworth. ■

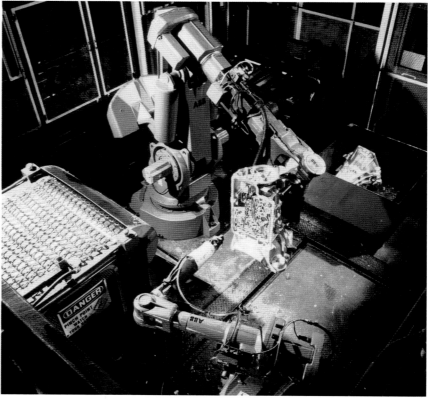

STATE-OF-THE-ART ROBOTICS IN A MULTI-STAGE CELL OPERATION.

SOBOTEC LTD.

Hamilton's Sobotec Ltd. is a young company that is helping to reverse the historical trade patterns with the United States. Rather than importing a finished product manufactured from Canadian raw materials, Sobotec is using local technology to add value to a U.S. raw material for export back to them. Almost three-quarters of its exports are to the United States.

Established in 1988 by two engineering graduates of McMaster University, brothers Vladimir and Chedo Sobot, Sobotec is one of the world's largest manufacturers of aluminum panel systems for use on the walls of commercial building projects. The raw material, Alucobond®,

is a pre-finished aluminum panel with a plastic core imported from the United States. This is a very cost-effective material that can be used to create highly complex shapes. It will stay very flat or it can be formed into a variety of unique shapes. One of its biggest features is its shiny high-tech visually appealing appearance that makes it ideal for use by companies that wish to project a new and modern image.

Sobotec engineers developed unique manufacturing systems that take that raw product and transform it into useable panels that can be installed on walls. Today, 90 per cent of company sales are attributed to its proprietary engineered dry joint systems. Panels can be installed without the need to caulk seal joints and it is one of the few firms on the market that is able to conceal all fasteners in its walls. This helps to further enhance the visual appearance of the final building product.

Sobotec operates from a modern state-of-the-art 40,000-square-feet manufacturing facility in Hamilton. Engineers utilize the latest in computer software for design, while manufacturing equipment is mainly computer controlled. This has enabled Sobotec to improve upon its quality and productivity while reducing costs. The majority of its engineers and technicians are graduates of either McMaster University or Mohawk College and Sobotec's installation crews travel all over eastern Canada to install its systems.

Sobotec is presently working on projects at Logan Airport in Boston as well as the airports in Cleveland and Cincinnati. It has been involved with projects in Chicago and Indianapolis and buildings such as the Marine Midland Arena in Buffalo and the Dearborn Police Station in Michigan. It works with national accounts programs for Mercedes, Honda, Acura and Ford and it is in the process of retrofitting all of the Petro-Canada stations throughout eastern and central Canada.

Sobotec's largest project to date has been the Windsor Casino. It was able to supply 375,000 square feet of panel within a mere 16 months. The casino project is, in fact, one of the largest applications of Alucobond material completed in North America. In addition to the Petro Canada stations, Sobotec's local work can be seen in the Reimer Corporate Centre in Burlington and the St. Joseph's Health Care Centre in Hamilton. ■

SOBOTEC IS ONE OF THE WORLD'S LARGEST MANUFACTURERS OF ALUMINUM PANEL SYSTEMS. THE RAW MATERIAL, ALUCOBOND, IS A PRE-FINISHED ALUMINUM PANEL WITH A PLASTIC CORE. CASINO WINDSOR, LOCATED IN WINDSOR, ONTARIO, IS ONE OF THE LARGEST AND MOST PRESTIGIOUS PROJECTS RECENTLY COMPLETED BY SOBOTEC. THIS PROJECT IS ONE OF THE LARGEST APPLICATIONS OF ALUCOBOND MATERIAL COMPLETED IN NORTH AMERICA. PHOTO BY ERIC OXENDORF.

CHAPTER 10

BUSINESS & PROFESSIONS

PHOTO BY MIKE GRANDMAISON.

NEW CITY OF HAMILTON

The coming year will be one of challenge for Hamilton and its neighbouring municipalities as it begins life as the newly amalgamated "super city"—the fourth largest city in Ontario with a population of 475,000 people. Success, however, is guaranteed thanks to the area's strong assets of an excellent location, available and reasonably priced industrial land, a highly skilled workforce and a quality of life that is second to none.

The traditional steel sector, the backbone of local industry, continues to expand with both Stelco and Dofasco making major improvements to their production facilities. Their presence has resulted in companies like Nova Steel, Taylor Steel, Nelson Steel and Walker National building large production plants in the area.

Partly because of Hamilton's proximity to good road, rail, water and air routes and its connection to major markets throughout Eastern North America, many firms have either moved into the area or expanded their local production. Tiercon Coatings opened a new 162,000-square-foot plant in Stoney Creek to coat plastic auto parts made by its sister firm located

nearby. Orlick Industries, another auto parts manufacturer, is planning significant expansions for its manufacturing near the rapidly growing John C. Munro Hamilton International Airport.

DURING THE PAST CENTURY HAMILTON HAS GROWN FROM A SMALL LAKEPORT TO A SPRAWLING URBAN CENTRE. AND THE NEW MILLENNIUM INTRODUCES MORE GROWTH AND CHANGE AS HAMILTON BEGINS LIFE AS THE NEW AMALGAMATED "SUPER CITY"—THE FOURTH-LARGEST CITY IN ONTARIO.

Arcor Windows is also expanding its production facilities in the city-owned 40-acre Techpark located at the junction of highways 5 and 6 partly because that puts it within a day's drive of 108 million customers. Nine new plants are presently being built there with five of them relocating to Hamilton from surrounding municipalities. In the same spot is the 40,000-square-foot city-owned and-operated Greater Hamilton Technology Enterprise Centre (GHTEC), which achieved 100 per cent occupancy in 1999 and became operationally self-sustaining.

GHTEC, with industries like robotics manufacturer Opus Automation, is an example of the diversity of the local economy that has expanded well beyond heavy industry. Thanks, in part, to a major university, a community college and first-class hospitals, Hamilton can train workers for employment in the rapidly expanding knowledge industries. Many of these graduates find employment in Hamilton and other qualified people are attracted to the city because of the new opportunities that exist.

The medical facilities and their affiliation with area hospitals have resulted in Hamilton becoming a major world centre for new drug development and testing. Aside from the economic impact, citizens are able to obtain first-class health care. The newly established e-commerce graduate training program in the business school and the existence of the new fibre-optic communication system (Fibrewired) will enable the city to expand e-commerce type businesses.

For the future, the Economic Development Department will be aggressively pursuing the Brownfield Redevelopment Strategy designed

IT IS NO WONDER HAMILTON'S TOURISM INDUSTRY IS FLOURISHING WITH SUCH BREATHTAKING MUSEUMS AS DUNDURN CASTLE, WHICH ALLOWS VISITORS TO EXPERIENCE LOCAL HISTORY FIRST HAND.

A new medicinal plant garden will be built at the Royal Botanical Gardens to explore the relationship between people and the plants they use for health and well-being. The existing waterfront facilities will be expanded to become even more of a "people place" with the potential development of a shopping/boutique area, restaurants and museums.

The downtown core is also undergoing improvements with the restoration of the old Spectator building, the train station, the Lister Block, new residential/commercial developments on King Street East and the grand opening of the City Place Apartments on King William Street.

The film industry is also expanding significantly and Hamilton is now host to dozens of feature film, television and music video productions.

Because of all the city has to offer, the International Cycling Union chose Hamilton to host the 2003 World Road Cycling Championships. Since 1927, this event has been held outside Europe only four times and only held in North America once. The event is anticipated to bring 1,500 athletes and half a million visitors to Hamilton along with an estimated $45 million in revenue and worldwide recognition for the city.

It is little wonder that in a recent study, Hamilton was judged to be the best place in Ontario to live. ◼

AS THE WATERFRONT AND DOWNTOWN HAMILTON AREAS UNDERGO EXPANSION AND REVITALIZATION, GORE PARK REMAINS A SYMBOL OF THE CITY'S INNOVATION AND COMMUNITY PRIDE.

to encourage development and investment of former industrial properties. This will include a Community Improvement Plan with provisions for incentives to increase development. The department will also begin work on the next three-year strategy for 2001 to 2003.

Tourism is not only a growing sector, but Hamilton's location and the natural beauty of the conservation lands greatly add to the quality of life for those who live here. Visitors to the city can enjoy the many trails that wind their way through the Royal Botanical Gardens or the Conservation Authority lands, visit the Art Gallery and museums like the Canadian Warplane Heritage Museum, Dundurn Castle and Whitehern. Bayfront Park, on the waterfront, is home to various festivals most summer weekends. Visitors can also use Hamilton as a hub and venture off to some of the Province's other tourist sites like the Niagara Region, St. Jacobs and Toronto, all of which are only an hour or two drive away. The tourism sector will also look at developing niche-marketing programs to attract tourists who enjoy golf, gardens, historical homes and architecture as well as those interested in ecology and agriculture.

Plans to improve upon the successes in the tourism sector involve a number of new projects. A Millennium Trail will tell the story of Hamilton's growth from a small mid-19th century lakeport to a sprawling 20th century urban centre. Visitors will learn about the city's evolution while travelling the trail either by foot, bicycle, car or public transit.

HAMILTON'S LOCATION AND ABUNDANCE OF NATURAL BEAUTY APPEALS TO VISITORS AND RESIDENTS ALIKE. HERE A YOUNG WOMAN ENJOYS THE LILACS IN THE ROYAL BOTANICAL GARDENS.

PRICEWATERHOUSECOOPERS LLP

PricewaterhouseCoopers is dedicated to providing its clients with the professional services they need for their business success. As the result of internal growth and a series of mergers, the most recent between PriceWaterhouse and Coopers & Lybrand in 1998, the Hamilton office has grown to seven partners and a staff of 100. The firm continues to enjoy a well-earned reputation for excellence, innovative client services and professional leadership.

As testimony to the multifaceted services it provides, PricewaterhouseCoopers points to its client base, which is comprised of emerging companies with exceptional growth potential, leading provincial and national companies, and some of the world's most complex organizations. This diversity is possible because staff members place a great deal of importance on understanding each business and the unique needs of those businesses, regardless of size. As a result, PricewaterhouseCoopers has maintained long term relationships with many of its clients, often over several generations of family-based businesses.

PricewaterhouseCoopers offers a comprehensive range of services in the following areas: Assurance and Business Advisory Services (including audit and attest services, support for mergers, acquisitions and divestitures); Financial Advisory Services (business recovery services, dispute analysis and investigations, corporate finance and investment banking services); and Tax Services (personal and corporate income tax services including estates and trusts, and commodity tax services). In all cases, the latest technology is utilized to assist in providing the best advice.

Because of its international presence, the company also is able to provide its local clients with appropriate expertise and experience, as required, of any one of its 150,000 professionals in its offices located in 150 countries around the world.

COMPANIES OF ALL SIZES RETAIN THE COMPREHENSIVE SERVICES OF INTERNATIONALLY KNOWN PRICEWATERHOUSECOOPERS.

The dispute analysis and investigations group has increased its business significantly. It provides creative solutions to assist in various insurance claim settlements, including those involving automobiles. It is also involved with the calculation of business interruption losses and the establishment of inventory existence. Several staff members act as expert witnesses in trials.

The Hamilton office recently established the Centre for Entrepreneurs and Family Business to better service entrepreneurs and their families. The Centre's mandate is to provide seamless delivery of tax planning and annual financial services to closely held corporations and business owners.

One of the unique features the Centre offers is succession and strategic planning services. Statistics indicate that less than one in three family businesses survive to the second generation, while only 10 per cent make it through to the third generation. These are very disturbing statistics, given that the majority of people hope their businesses will carry on after them. There are two main causes for this high rate of succession failure. The first is the absence of a plan that results in succession being left to a combination of chance and succession laws. The second is the development of plans without regard for the personal objectives of each member of the family. At the Centre, PricewaterhouseCoopers' experts meet with all members of the family, including those not involved in the company, as well as key employees to determine objectives. Once the objectives have been defined and full information received, plans and policies can be developed.

PARTNERS AND STAFF WORK TOGETHER TO PROVIDE PRACTICAL SOLUTIONS TO THEIR CLIENTS' PROBLEMS.

Frequently, founders plan for succession in isolation from the rest of the family and without a full understanding of the needs and intentions of others. As well, founders are occasionally focused on minimizing taxes without fully considering the impact of their tax plan on the family dynamic and the future of the business. Staff of the Centre not only provide appropriate information, but also work with the family members to ensure that each individual's objectives are satisfied and that, from a business perspective, the plans are reasonable and attainable. This enables the owner to implement a plan that will help to ensure the continuation of their successful achievements while, at the same time, promoting family harmony and the satisfaction of the goals of the other family members.

Estates, trusts and compensation planning are other examples of growing areas, especially as baby boomers age. The firm's specialists focus on minimizing taxes at death, transferring growth to the next generation, income splitting among family members and developing a compensation plan for shareholders based on their specific circumstances.

In addition to these services, the Centre also offers an extensive Resource and Learning Centre for its clients' use.

As an employer, PricewaterhouseCoopers is committed to helping its staff and partners achieve a balance in their professional and personal goals. Its flexible work arrangements program helps staff to become more creative and

THE FIRM IS COMMITTED TO CONTINUOUS LEARNING AND EDUCATION.

more effective in changing, adapting and improving the way they work. Non-traditional ways of working are supported, where practical, in order to retain valued staff who need or want a more flexible arrangement.

As a corporate citizen, the staff and partners of the firm are actively involved with the community. PricewaterhouseCoopers is a major sponsor of local events such as the Hamilton and District Chamber of Commerce Outstanding Business Achievement Awards. In addition, staff and partners are very active with a variety of charities, including McMaster University, the Hamilton Community Foundation, local hospitals, arts and other organizations.

PricewaterhouseCoopers is committed to providing consistent, high-quality service to its clients in the Hamilton area, Canada and throughout the world. Its vision is to be the best professional services firm in the world, as measured by the markets and clients it serves and by its people. ■

PRICEWATERHOUSECOOPERS HAS PROVIDED A WIDE RANGE OF PROFESSIONAL SERVICES TO AREA BUSINESSES FOR SEVERAL GENERATIONS.

HAMILTON AND DISTRICT CHAMBER OF COMMERCE

The Hamilton and District Chamber of Commerce has been "creating business opportunities" for its members since 1845. Today, this broadly based organization, which reflects the make-up of the economic structure of the community, is a place where entrepreneurs who work out of their home offices have an opportunity to rub shoulders with executives from the area's largest employers and to network with a wide cross section of other business people.

As for the economy, Hamilton is still a "city that makes things." Much of the economic growth has been in smaller companies rather than amongst U.S. subsidiaries or in steel. Employment in the primary metals industry, the backbone and still an important part of the economy, has declined from 33 per cent to 23 per cent of the local labour force. Small- to medium-sized manufacturers are benefitting from NAFTA by finding specialized niche manufacturing opportunities. Thanks to free trade, 60 per cent of the local GDP is based on exports, with 80 per cent of those exports going to the U.S.

The activities of the Chamber have been changing to reflect this shift in business and to address the current needs of its members. It is now focusing more on issues of international trade and strategies to improve transportation, communication and cost reduction, which are essential for the success of local businesses.

The Chamber has an active committee structure that enables its members to become involved and to contribute to the development of policy at the city, provincial and federal levels. There are 15 standing committees active in the organization and half of these advocate on policy issues on behalf of members. Well over 300 Chamber members contribute their time to these endeavors that bring important, well-thought-out issues on behalf of the community as a whole to the appropriate level of government. Few small businesses would be able to afford the research and advocacy services they get from the Chamber committees for the cost of their annual membership.

In addition to the committee work, the Chamber puts on about 80 events for members. Many of these are at no additional cost such as the monthly Business After Business networking meeting. At these events, members get an opportunity to visit the host firm and to mingle with colleagues.

CHAMBER MEMBERS ENJOYING ONE OF THE MANY FUNCTIONS HELD AT "THE CHAMBER CLUB" ON HAMILTON'S WATERFRONT. PHOTO BY DAVID GRUGGEN PHOTOGRAPHY.

The Chamber is the largest and oldest chamber of commerce in the area, predating both the City of Hamilton and all of its member companies. It presently has 1,700 members from 1,150 different companies who employ over 75,000 full-time employees. What is unique about the organization is that it truly reflects the composition of employers in the city by pursuing a diversified approach to recruitment.

The Chamber includes among its membership hospitals, school boards, police services, government, not for profit organizations and a union. Most of the major employers in Hamilton belong and the organization has doubled in size in the past five years.

Over the past three years, there has been a significant growth in small home-based businesses and that is reflected in membership. Businesses employing fewer than 10 people have grown to comprise 72 per cent of Chamber members, while those with fewer than 4 staff persons account for 40 per cent of the membership. Membership in the Chamber does reflect the economic mix of the city.

NETWORKING IS A PRIORITY WITH MANY CHAMBER MEMBERS AND THE ORGANIZATION GIVES THEM AS MANY OPPORTUNITIES AS POSSIBLE TO DO JUST THAT.

There are also monthly breakfast meetings and regular new member receptions. Twice a year, it hosts a small business showcase along with numerous seminars, educational opportunities and dinners. The Chamber also recognizes successes in the community by organizing annual Citizen of the Year and Youth Volunteer of the Year awards in Hamilton, Dundas and Ancaster. Members also have an opportunity to join networking groups within the Chamber to expand their contacts.

Friends or business associates can be entertained in the private dining room with its spectacular view looking out over the bay and yacht club. For those travelling, reciprocal privileges are available in the facilities of other Chambers and Boards of Trade. Of particular interest to the small and home-based business entrepreneurs is the insurance savings that are offered to members. Chamber members can access the Chambers of Commerce of Canada Group Insurance Plan that provides features like life, health and long-term disability coverage.

The Chamber recently conducted a telephone survey of about 70 per cent of its members and asked them to rate their satisfaction with their membership on a scale of 1 to 10 with 10 being the highest satisfaction. The organization was rated at 7.9. For new members, networking was the main reason they listed for joining, but they also stated that business advocacy was a valuable service provided for them by the Chamber.

The Hamilton Chamber is also only one of three Chambers in Canada to be licensed to administer the Athena Award by the international Athena Foundation. This is an award presented to those who have helped mentor women in business and the professions. It is also a founding partner in establishing a Hamilton Safe Communities Coalition in the region.

That bodes well for the Chamber's latest venture: To improve the communications capabilities of its members by using the new high-speed fibre-optic network now available in the city. Member profiles will be on-line and the Chamber will be able to establish Virtual Private Networks or VPNs for members using this latest high-speed technology. This new venture is a reflection of the Chamber's belief that modern businesses and entrepreneurs must learn to embrace and rapidly adapt to the quickly changing world of technology. ◼

HUNDREDS OF THE COMMUNITY'S BUSINESS LEADERS GATHER EACH YEAR AT THE CHAMBER'S "OUTSTANDING BUSINESS ACHIEVEMENT AWARDS" TO RECOGNIZE THE SUCCESS OF THEIR PEERS IN LARGE, SMALL, YOUNG ENTREPRENEUR OF THE YEAR AND IRONMAN CATEGORIES. PHOTO BY WAVELENGTH.

THE CHAMBER IS THE RECOGNIZED "VOICE OF BUSINESS" IN HAMILTON AND IS REGULARLY SOUGHT OUT TO COMMENT ON SIGNIFICANT COMMUNITY ISSUES. PHOTO BY WAVELENGTH.

WORDCRAFT COMMUNICATIONS

Jerry Amernic is a public relations consultant and journalist. A graduate of the University of Toronto, he began his career as a newspaper reporter and later joined the corporate communications department of IBM Canada. Since 1979, he has been active as a skilled professional who offers journalistic, editorial, public relations and training services. Jerry has been a columnist with a major daily newspaper, has written several books and is a frequent contributor to magazines, newspapers and trade journals. He is also a keynote speaker and leader of workshops and seminars; his subjects include communications in the world of business, dealing with media relationships and raising profile and how to improve written communications in particular.

For several years he has been an instructor in the Public Relations Program at Humber College of Applied Arts and Technology in Toronto and at Seneca College of Applied Arts in Technology, also in Toronto. As a specialist in his industry, Jerry conducts communications programs for consultants in public relations and marketing companies and for the business community in general. These programs involve professional public relations, the specifics behind media relations, internal corporate communications and how to improve written communications. In addition, he conducts media-training sessions for executives.

Through his company Wordcraft Communications, he has worked with many leading corporations from a variety of sectors including high-tech (Northern Telecom, Honeywell, NCR, Bull); financial services (Bank of Montreal, Investors Group, Dynamic Mutual Funds); health care (Glaxo Wellcome, Extendicare) and consulting (Andersen Consulting). He has also worked with small entrepreneurial organizations, associations and government. Jerry has been a speechwriter for business leaders and also a number of Ontario Government Cabinet Ministers. A media-relations specialist, he is an expert at generating print and electronic media exposure on behalf of clients. He plans and manages news conferences and corporate launches, develops strategies for crisis communications and produces such corporate publications as annual reports and newsletters.

Jerry is the author of two books for Community Communications—*Markham: Shaping a Destiny*, which was published in 1998, and *Canada's Technology Triangle: An Economic Celebration*, which was published in 1999. He is also the author of the book *Victims: The Orphans of Justice*, published by Bantam in 1984. ∎

JERRY AMERNIC.

CHAPTER 11

CONSTRUCTION & UTILITIES

PHOTO BY MIKE GRANDMAISON.

HAMILTON UTILITIES CORPORATION

From the horse-drawn carts of the early years to the computerized control systems and fibre optics of today, the citizens of Hamilton benefit from one of the most efficient hydro systems in the province. Hamilton Hydro's goal has always been to safely provide a reliable supply of electricity along with value-added services at competitive rates and in an efficient and environmentally responsible manner.

Its goal is indicative still through the Corporate Vision— to be recognized as the leader in the delivery of municipal utility services with its customers saying they are receiving best value.

In 1937, the *Hamilton Spectator* wrote that Hamilton Hydro "has won the envious distinction of being the most efficiently operated in Ontario...particularly in regards to cost to the users...." During the rapid expansion following World War II, most communities in Ontario experienced blackouts, but not Hamilton. The *Globe and Mail* reported that "in a province beset by dim-outs and power cutoffs, the City of Hamilton stands out as an oasis of light."

Hamilton, in fact, was originally known as The Electric City because it so rapidly adopted electric power in the 1880s. Then, power was supplied by private companies. Because of this abundant source of cheap power, many industrial firms began production in Hamilton. In the 1890s, there was a demand from some citizens to establish a municipally run electric system. Hydro began in 1912 with five customers and was run by a committee of the City Board of Control. In 1914, the management of Hamilton Hydro was changed to a Commission elected directly by the voters.

From Hydro's very beginning, its customers have benefited from extremely low rates compared to other communities or to its private competition. In 1912, a private customer paid $2.49 for 30 Kw hours/month compared to $1.21 for Hydro. By 1919, the Ontario Hydro Commission reported that "Hamilton now enjoys the distinction of having the cheapest lighting and power rates of any city on the continent...."

55 JOHN STREET NORTH—HAMILTON UTILITIES CORPORATION HEAD OFFICE. THIS BUILDING OPENED IN 1951 WITH THREE FLOORS, AND THE REMAINING THREE WERE ADDED BY 1960. THE BUILDING NOW HOUSES 157 EMPLOYEES IN BILLING, CUSTOMER SERVICE, ACCOUNTING, METERING, ENGINEERING, INFORMATION SYSTEMS AND OPERATING DEPARTMENTS.

In 1926, the distribution of energy in Toronto cost $15.40 per consumer compared to only $6.10 in Hamilton.

This early, rapid and inexpensive source of power helped fuel the industrialization of the city. According to a local paper writing in those early days of development, "As Hydro grows, so does Hamilton in population and industrial production." Today, Hamilton Hydro is entering into an era of deregulation in the electrical industry and a return to competition, but it does so with the intent to continue with the same successful format that it has used since its inception.

Presently, the utility has about 170,000 customers and 325 staff and, based on peak load, is the third largest municipal electric utility in Ontario. It handles all of the electrical distribution within the City of Hamilton along with the design and construction of underground ducts and pole lines. Hydro is also responsible for all aspects of the city street lighting.

Hydro prides itself on its responsiveness to its customers, whether in its rebuilding in an area to improve reliability or in maintaining a 24-hour-a-day trouble crew to handle emergencies. It recently completed computerizing all engineering records in order to improve accuracy and to provide more consistent detail in the information needed to run the organization. The new computerized Supervisory Control and Data Acquisition (SCADA) system enables staff to constantly monitor the status of electrical circuits throughout the city. The Operating Department is immediately alerted to any abnormality in the electrical system enabling Hydro to dispatch a trouble crew to the site in the shortest possible time.

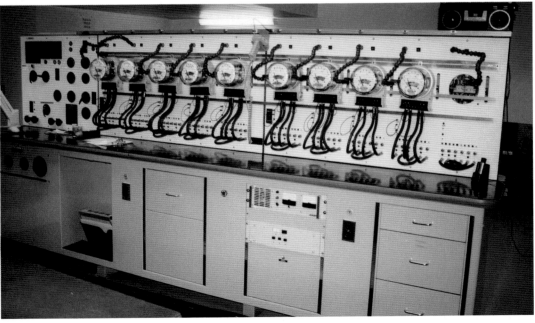

A VIEW OF ONE OF THE FOUR METERING TEST BOARDS IN HAMILTON HYDRO'S ACCREDITED METER SHOP. THE TEST BOARD IS USED TO RE-VERIFY ELECTRICAL METERS FOR HAMILTON HYDRO AND OTHER METER SERVICE ORGANIZATION CLIENTS.

UNDERGROUND CABLES—IN DUCTS OR DIRECT BURIED—ARE INSTALLED BY HAMILTON HYDRO'S SKILLED UNDERGROUND CONSTRUCTION CREWS. AN EXTENSIVE UNDERGROUND SYSTEM PROVIDES "OUT-OF-SIGHT" ELECTRICAL SERVICE TO RESIDENTIAL, COMMERCIAL AND INDUSTRIAL CUSTOMERS THROUGHOUT THE CITY.

Since the 1930s, Hydro has had its own internal communication system that has recently been upgraded to fibre optics. The excess capacity available from this system is being made available to other businesses in the region through FibreWired, a Hamilton Utilities Company. This network of fibre optic cables provides the platform for an advanced communications network that stretches across Hamilton and its borders, while reaching around the globe.

FibreWired is providing Hamilton Hydro and local businesses with the highest-speed voice and data communications to connect remote offices to each other and to the entire world, to provide off-site data storage, high-speed internet access and high-speed virtual private networks. This system is being offered to all schools in the region so children can learn on the fastest network available today with access to new multimedia learning tools and educational material.

Another accomplishment has been the accreditation of the meter shop from the Canadian Bureau of Measurement. Hamilton Hydro's standards for processing meters meet the requirements established by the Canadian government. This recognition of quality means that the utility offers meter sealing services as well as installations, which has resulted in it providing services to hydro companies in other communities, thus generating revenue for the corporation.

Hydro has an extensive fleet of 90 vehicles ranging from the typical small vans to a 300-Kw trailer-mounted generator. There are 65-foot double-bucket trucks, a cable-pulling truck and a vacuum truck used for digging holes. This ensures that Hydro is able to handle all aspects of electrical installation and maintenance.

Now a community-owned utility company, Hamilton Utilities Corporation has been formed from the five previous municipal electricity utilities, Ancaster, Dundas, Flamborough, Hamilton and Stoney Creek. It is structured to provide a broad range of utility services, initially through three operating companies: Hamilton Hydro Inc., FibreWired and Hamilton Community Energy. ■

INSTALLATION AND MAINTENANCE OF THE MANY KILOMETERS OF OVERHEAD LINES THROUGHOUT HAMILTON IS SAFER AND FASTER WITH THE USE OF AERIAL BUCKET TRUCKS. THE TRUCK PICTURED ABOVE CAN SAFELY TAKE QUALIFIED LINEMEN TO HEIGHTS OF 65 FEET FOR THEM TO WORK ON 13,000-VOLT LINES.

ANDREE'S MAINTENANCE

"Fueling into the future" is the motto of Andree's Maintenance Ltd., which has been specializing in the petroleum and construction areas from its Dundas location for more than 10 years. In addition to providing the traditional turnkey underground fuel tank systems, Andree's provides a unique and environmentally safe aboveground tank system along with the only leasing plan in the industry.

Environmental safety is an ever-increasing concern, and Andree's above ground systems solve those problems. Older underground tanks used for petroleum, fuel oil, waste oil and chemicals always run the risk of leaking over time and contaminating the soil. Insurance costs for owners can be higher because of the dangers of contamination, and land values can be depressed. When there is an underground tank on a piece of land, the value of the property may decline because of the possibility that the tank has leaked and contaminated the soil. This environmental damage cannot be ignored but must be repaired. That may result in considerable cost to the owner.

This is not a problem with Andree's above ground tank systems. The storeage tanks are not buried but sit above the ground on a platform. All tanks are of double-walled steel construction and have fill/spill collectors to prevent spills. Tanks meet and exceed local and federal safety expectations and are guaranteed by the manufacturer for 25 years. Tanks are designed to meet the specific requirements and needs of the individual customer and his or her particular application. Tanks range in size and can be as large as 100,000 litres. They can even be fitted with a fixed steel ladder for maintenance and inspection.

Of course, Andree's also will design and install underground systems for those who require that service. All underground tanks are made with double walls and have spill containment devices fitted to them. There is also an overfill protection device with an electronic audible/visible alarm, as well as emergency venting that meets all environmental requirements and a leak-detection system.

Andree's staff is available to help build, upgrade or add to an existing facility. They can put their professionalism to work for customers desiring gas bars, water treatment facilities and fueling facilities. Not only are they bonded but they are fully licensed for fuel safety by the Ministry of the Environment and Energy.

Andree's is also able to offer what no other tank supplier can—custom leases that provide its customers with the flexibility that they need for their businesses. In partnership with Newcourt Leasing, packages are offered for all sizes of aboveground tanks. Leases can include pumps, card locks, fuel management systems, guard rails, lighting and other options that might be applicable to the customized system. The lease includes everything to ensure a complete turnkey operation. In addition, each tank comes with a $2-million environmental insurance policy.

The lease also includes transportation to the site by truck, rail, ferry, air or whatever other special means might be required. The length of the lease is negotiable and is designed to fit in with a company's specific business needs. The standard lease normally runs for five years with a $10 buyout at the end of the term, but special requirements can be factored into any lease. Andree's guarantees that it will not be undersold.

The Andree's turnkey system provides everything for the customer. All they need to do is to provide Andree's staff with their requirements and the power to run their system. Andree's own staff, combined with

their alliances with other professionals, will plan and complete all aspects of a job. They will help design a new project and build or renovate based on the customer's own plans.

Through its alliances with engineers and consulting firms, Andree's can assist its customers through all phases of construction. Andree's also owns and operates construction equipment to provide any demolition that might be required by a customer and to perform any needed paving for the project. The goal of the Andree's management and service specialists is to maintain their proven leadership and to strive for the highest standard.

In fact, Andree's Management takes pride in giving cost-effective and innovative solutions to all petroleum areas and bringing all projects to a successful close. Its goal is to provide quality petroleum service in a timely manner and at a fair price while exceeding the expectations of its clients. Andree's understands its clients' priorities and problems and strives to build a working relationship with them based on mutual trust and respect.

No job is too big or too small for Andree's. Its customers range from small independent firms to large major oil companies, trucking firms, corporations in a variety of businesses and government. The Andree's aboveground tank systems are ideal for fleet owners, greenhouse growers, forestry operations, marina operations, industrial/commercial applications and governments at all levels for the storage of petroleum, fuel oil, waste oil and chemicals.

Most of the systems are delivered within continental North America but Andree's can and does provide service worldwide.

COMPLETELY PORTABLE ABOVEGROUND FUELING CENTRE, COMPLETE WITH SPLIT TANKS, HIGH-SPEED FUEL PUMPS, LIGHTING, GUARD RAIL AND 24-HOUR CARD LOCK.

Quotes can be given by fax or by electronic mail but Andree's is also the only company in the petroleum contracting field to employ sales staff. They can assist potential clients to customize their needs and can then provide a quote based on those unique requirements. ■

RETAIL GAS BAR. BUILT TO MEET AND EXCEED THE CUSTOMER'S EXPECTATIONS AND REQUIREMENTS. ANDREE'S DELIVERS A TURNKEY OPERATION.

LABOURER'S INTERNATIONAL UNION OF NORTH AMERICA

Amongst labour unions, LIUNA stands out as a unique and innovative organization that understands business and works with those businesses to help create jobs both for its own members and for the community it serves. LIUNA was founded in 1903 although the Hamilton Local Union, Local 837, was not formed until the 1940s.

LIUNA LOCAL 837'S HEAD OFFICE ON HUGHSON STREET SOUTH ALSO HOUSES THE OFFICE OF THE CANADIAN DIRECTOR AND THE CENTRAL AND EASTERN CANADA REGIONAL OFFICE.

Today, Local 837 represents over 3,000 members who work in various sectors including construction, health care and the school boards. The majority of its members build the roads, sewers, bridges, hospitals and schools, while its other members work in those schools and hospitals and serve the citizens of the city. Hamilton is also home to the Regional and Canadian headquarters for the union.

LIUNA has an impeccable reputation with employers as an innovator in labour relations thanks to its philosophy of employer/employee cooperation for the benefit of both. Union officials strive for a win/win situation in their contract negotiations.

The union has a very strong commitment to the community as is evidenced by the numerous projects it has in Hamilton to help revitalize the city and to create jobs.

In 1982, it established LIUNA Gardens on the shores of Lake Ontario in Stoney Creek. This 11-acre complex is an award-winning banquet and conference facility that services all groups locally and in the Niagara Peninsula. A year earlier in 1981, the organization entered the social housing field. Today, LIUNA has one of the largest portfolios of affordable housing units in Ontario and operates 600 homes for seniors, the disabled and low-income families.

One of the union's most ambitious projects has been the renovation of the abandoned CN train station. LIUNA Station is a new banquet and conference facility that complements the Gardens and serves the downtown area. The Station has been restored into two banquet halls, recreation facilities for LIUNA members and retirees, as well as commercial office space. The park area in front of the station is known as Immigration Square and recognizes the contributions to the country of the thousands of people who immigrated to Canada and who arrived through the Station.

LIUNA Station has already begun to revitalize the city's northern corridor. It provides jobs to people in the area during the day in addition to those who utilize the banquet facilities in the evenings and on the weekend. Furthermore, during the construction and renovation period, jobs were created for the rebuilding of the station, while many new permanent full- and part-time jobs have also resulted from the refurbishing of this structure.

Not far from the Station, the union is building a 120-bed long-term facility and day-care centre on previously contaminated factory land known as "brownfields," which the union recently reclaimed. LIUNA lobbies extensively on this issue with all levels of government and is acting as an example to demonstrate what can be accomplished by serious urban renewal efforts through this project.

This new complex at Queen and Napier streets is providing much needed construction jobs as well as bringing more permanent jobs into the downtown. The long-term-care facility and day-care centre to be administered by the YWCA will allow seniors to interact with the children for the benefit of both. It is also providing much needed long-term-care beds and day-care spaces.

LIUNA also partners with other groups to help bring more investment into the area. It has plans to preserve the historical facade of the derelict Lister Block on James Street North. It is also leading a consortium to purchase the Royal Connaught Hotel and upgrade the facility to a five-star hotel so that the hotel can resume its historical role as one of the finest in Canada.

ONE OF THE UNION'S MOST AMBITIOUS PROJECTS HAS BEEN THE RENOVATION OF THE ABANDONED CN TRAIN STATION INTO A BANQUET AND CONFERENCE FACILITY. PICTURED HERE IS LIUNA STATION'S GRAND OPENING ON MAY 27, 2000.

LIUNA Local 837 members marching in the 1999 Labour Day Parade.

LIUNA is also one of the original founding partners in Tradeport International which operates the John C. Munro, Hamilton International Airport. This was the first airport in Canada to be privatized and is considered to be one of the greatest business success stories in the area. In only three years, this under-utilized facility has become the premier cargo-handling facility for all of Eastern Canada. It is also rapidly becoming a busy passenger airport and a viable alternative to the Toronto airport. Three airlines now have regular daily flights from Hamilton and more carriers are planning to operate from the airport.

Recently, LIUNA became the only union to join the Hamilton and District Chamber of Commerce in the Chamber's 155-year history. This move reflects LIUNA's understanding of the business community and its desire to continue to partner with business for the continued well-being of its members and the community as a whole. ■

LIUNA Local 837, Executive Board Members, from left: Back row: Nicolo Scibetta, executive board member; Riccardo Persi, recording secretary; Lorenzo Curto, vice president; Pasquale Zavarella, executive board member. Front row: Manuel Bastos, business manager; Enrico Mancinelli, president; Joseph Mancinelli, secretary treasurer.

LAFARGE

Lafarge Canada, Inc. is a "small" large company. Even though it is part of a worldwide organization established in France over 160 years ago, does business in 65 countries and employs over 65,000 people, it still focuses on the community in which its employees live and work. Lafarge is proud to be both a part of the Region Hamilton-Wentworth and a responsible member of the business community. Its customers, from the private homeowner to the government, all receive the same high level of courteous service and quality materials.

Internationally, Lafarge is the number one producer of roofing materials and aluminates in the world and the second largest producer of cement, concrete and aggregates. Locally, it is very much an integral part of the construction industry through its construction division and in the supply of numerous construction materials for others. It is doubtful that there is anyone in the region who is not familiar with its distinctive "green L" corporate logo, seen on its many trucks and construction signs. The firm is proud of its commitment to improve the local infrastructure.

Lafarge is one of the largest ready-mixed concrete suppliers in the region. The Dundas Limestone Quarry is Canada's second largest quarry and produces crushed stone for road building, landscape stone and an array of other products. Since 1953, it has been processing blast-furnace slag for road bases, fills, lightweight masonry and concrete and roofing

ONE OF MANY READYMIX CONCRETE TRUCKS SERVING THE HAMILTON AREA.

materials at its innovative Slag Plant. Slag is also used as a raw material for wool insulation and slag cement. One-million tons are produced annually and the company has recently introduced a new lighter aggregate that improves fire resistance and sound attenuation.

Lafarge processes and markets all the slag produced by the Hamilton blast furnaces at both Stelco and Dofasco.

The construction division does roadwork for municipal, industrial, commercial and residential customers. In 1998, Lafarge was honoured with the Regional Paver of the Year Award from the Ontario Ministry of Transportation. This prestigous award was in recognition of the quality and workmanship demonstrated by Lafarge for paving Highway 403 west of Brantford.

The Workplace Safety and Insurance Board has recognized the firm for its dedication to workplace safety. The Slag Plant has operated for more than five years while the Dundas Quarry has logged over one-million man-hours without losing time to a work place injury.

This safety record reflects Lafarge's commitment to its employees (as well as to the community) and is a living example of its core values of quality, trust and teamwork. A commitment to its employees, customers, community and to innovation and excellence is the foundation for success at Lafarge. ■

LAFARGE CONSTRUCTION PAVING A LOCAL RESIDENTIAL STREET.

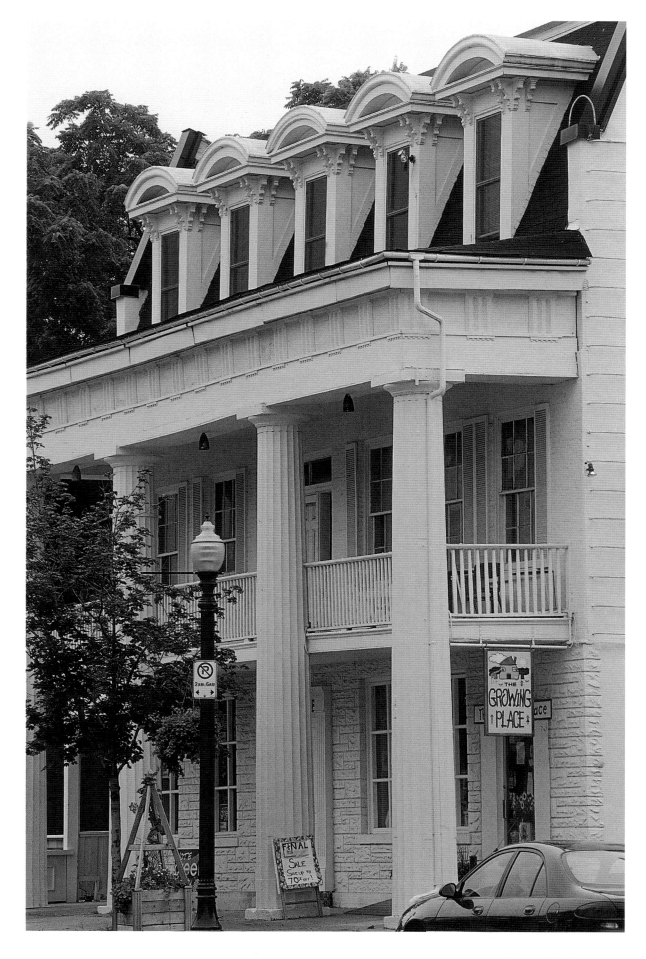

PHOTO BY MIKE GRANDMAISON.

ENTERPRISE INDEX

AMCAN CASTINGS LIMITED
9 Hillyard Street
Hamilton, Ontario L8L 6B2
Phone: 905-681-0747
Fax: 905-527-6542
www.amcancastings.com
Pages 108-109

ANDREE'S MAINTENANCE
1129 Highway #5 West RR#2
Dundas, Ontario L9H 5E2
Phone: 905-628-5868
Fax: 905-628-4655
E-mail: andrees.com@sympatico.ca
www.andrees.ca
Pages 126-127

DOFASCO
Box 2460
Hamilton, Ontario L8N 3J5
Phone: 905-548-7200 ext. 2200
Toll-free: 800-363-2726
Fax: 905-548-4935
E-mail: gordon_forstner@dofasco.ca
www.dofasco.ca
Pages 106-107

**HAMILTON AND DISTRICT
CHAMBER OF COMMERCE**
555 Bay Street North
Hamilton, Ontario L8L 1H1
Phone: 905-522-1151
Fax: 905-522-1154
E-mail: hdcc@hamilton-cofc.on.ca
www.hamilton-cofc.on.ca
Pages 118-119

**HAMILTON HEALTH SCIENCES
CORPORATION**
1200 Main Street West
Hamilton, Ontario L8N 3Z5
Phone: 905-521-2100 ext. 75387
Fax: 905-521-5090
E-mail: publicaffairs@hhsc.ca
www.hhsc.ca
Pages 96-97

**HAMILTON UTILITIES
CORPORATION**
55 John Street North
Hamilton, Ontario L8N 3E4
Phone: 905-317-4707
Fax: 905-522-6570
E-mail: cwupton@hamiltonhydro.com
www.hamiltonhydro.com
Pages 124-125

**HILLFIELD-STRATHALLAN
COLLEGE**
299 Fennell Avenue West
Hamilton, Ontario L9C 1G3
Phone: 905-389-1367
Fax: 905-389-6366
E-mail: admissions@hillstrath.on.ca
www.hillstrath.on.ca
Pages 92-93

**LABOURER'S INTERNATIONAL
UNION OF NORTH AMERICA**
44 Hughson Street South
Hamilton, Ontario L8N 2A7
Phone: 905-529-1116
Fax: 905-529-2723
E-mail: laborers837.on.ca
Pages 128-129

LAFARGE
525 Victoria Avenue North
PO Box 65, Depot #1
Hamilton, Ontario L8L 7V1
Phone: 905-522-1361
Fax: 905-522-7565
www.lcmeast.com
Page 130

MCMASTER UNIVERSITY
1280 Main Street West
Hamilton, Ontario L8S 4L8
Phone: 905-525-9140
Fax: 905-521-1504
www.mcmaster.ca
Pages 90-91

MOHAWK COLLEGE
135 Fennell Avenue West
PO Box 2034
Hamilton, Ontario L8N 3T2
Phone: 905-575-1212
Fax: 905-575-2378
www.mohawkc.on.ca
Pages 88-89

NEW CITY OF HAMILTON
1 James Street South, Suite 800
Hamilton, Ontario L8P 4R5
Phone: 905-546-4447
Fax: 905-546-4107
E-mail: ncatalan@hamilton-went.on.ca
www.hamilton-went.on.ca
Pages 114-115

PRICEWATERHOUSECOOPERS LLP
21 King Street West
Hamilton, Ontario L8P 4W7
Phone: 905-777-7000
Fax: 905-777-7060
www.pwcglobal.com/ca
Pages 116-117

ST. JOSEPH'S HOSPITAL
50 Charlton Avenue East
Hamilton, Ontario L8N 4A6
Phone: 905-522-1155
Fax: 905-540-6531
E-mail: jgarrett@stjosham.on.ca
www.stjosham.on.ca
Page 100

ST. JOSEPH'S VILLA
56 Governor's Road
Dundas, Ontario L9H 5G7
Phone: 905-627-9011
Fax: 905-628-0825
E-mail: stjvilla@interlynx.net
www.sjv.on.ca
Page 101

ST. PETER'S HEALTH SYSTEM
88 Maplewood Avenue
Hamilton, Ontario L8M 1W9
Phone: 905-549-6525
Fax: 905-545-0822
www.stpetershealthsystem.com
Pages 98-99

SOBOTEC LTD.
67 Burford Road
Hamilton, Ontario L8E 3C6
Phone: 905-578-1278
Fax: 905-578-1446
E-mail: vsobot@sobotec.com
www.sobotec.com
Page 110

TUBE-MAC® INDUSTRIES
853 Arvin Avenue
Stoney Creek, Ontario L8E 5N8
Phone: 905-643-8823
Fax: 905-643-0643
E-mail: info@tube-mac.com
www.tube-mac.com
Pages 104-105

**WORDCRAFT
COMMUNICATIONS**
341 Beechgrove Drive
Scarborough, Ontario M1E 4A2
Phone: 416-284-0838
Fax: 416-284-6202
E-mail: jerry.amernic@sympatico.ca
www3.sympatico.ca/jerry.amernic
Page 120

INDEX